INSIDE *your* DREAMS

INSIDE
your
DREAMS

An advanced guide to your
night visions

ROSE INSERRA

ROCKPOOL

A dream that is not understood remains a mere occurrence; understood it becomes a living experience.

– CARL JUNG

A Rockpool book
PO Box 252
Summer Hill
NSW 2130
Australia

rockpoolpublishing.co
Follow us! **f** ☉ rockpoolpublishing
Tag your images with #rockpoolpublishing

ISBN: 9781925924503

Published in 2021 by Rockpool Publishing

Editing and index by Lisa Macken
Proofread by Gumhill proofreading
Design and typesetting by Sara Lindberg, Rockpool Publishing

 A catalogue record for this book is available from the National Library of Australia

Printed and bound in China
10 9 8 7 6 5 4 3 2 1

CONTENTS

DREAM
YOUR LIFE
INTO LIFE.

FOLLOW
YOUR
DREAMS
... THEY
KNOW
THE WAY.

INTRODUCTION

Since the beginning of time we've wondered about our dreams and their strange symbolic language, which has intrigued, frightened, informed and inspired humanity. We've come a long way from superstitious beliefs: when seeing a snake was a bad omen that meant you'd be betrayed, or losing your teeth was a sign that a family member was going to die.

The tradition of sharing dreams goes all the way back to Emperor Augustus (63 BCE–14 CE), who ordered Roman citizens to share their dreams if the dreams had anything to do with Rome. This decree came about because the emperor was saved by a dream in which he was told to leave his tent just before he was attacked. Dreaming was thus highly regarded, as it also was in the ancient civilisations of Mesopotamia, Egypt and Greece and in Celtic, indigenous and pagan traditions.

I was born in a small town 170 km south of Rome and was fortunate to be surrounded by a rich tradition and belief system that respected the old pagan ways that pre-dated Christianity. Dreaming was seen as being significant and had to be shared, especially if it was disturbing. My grandmother and aunt would take any of my dreams seriously and would take *me* seriously, which helped me to feel connected to my heritage. In many cultures sharing dreams is encouraged and is often a duty to the village, as it is for the benefit of everyone in the village that the dream is interpreted. The ancients trusted their deep wisdom and intuition, which often came as a result of interpreting their dreams and acting on the insights gained in those dreams.

Unfortunately, we've lost the tradition of sharing dreams, although it is just as important now as it was previously and is essential to the survival of the collective tribe we call humanity. Our dreams link us to the collective unconscious, or the shared structures of the unconscious mind. We are not so different, after all, if we share the same or similar dreams.

This book was written for the everyday reader who may or may not be a dreamer. Outside the borderlands of dreaming you will learn other valuable tools on your journey to self-awareness and spiritual knowledge. My greatest wish is to invite you into a journey of endless possibilities so you can expand into deeper dimensions of consciousness. It's ambitious, but not improbable.

Collectively we have entered a cataclysmic time . . . unlike the ancients, who believed they lived only by the whim of the gods. Mother Earth has unleashed her fury via bush fires, floods, drought, faunal and floral extinction and a global pandemic, and although we have placed all our faith in science to protect us we are now questioning that faith. What is science doing to help us?

We live in a world of ecological crisis and know as human beings we must make changes. Now is the time to alter our interactions with Mother Earth and allow her to regenerate, so we humans and the planet can thrive once more. These times offer a unique opportunity to reflect, create and reconnect with core values and strengthen familial bonds, and to foster independence, resilience, resourcefulness, innovation and creativity. How will we move from these liminal times? Although we are experiencing a dark night of the soul, we know that night always turns back into day.

The big picture theme of this book is 'collective dreaming'. I never cease to be amazed at the similarities of our dreams, and it fascinates me to study the variations, synchronicities, cultural history, archetypal dream journeys, humanity's indigenous knowledge systems and conscious dreaming and all the wisdom they bring to our 21st-century mindset.

HOW TO USE THE BOOK

You may wish to adopt a dip-in approach whereby you read particular chapters of the book depending on your level of interest and energy, or you might prefer to treat the book as a practical manual and read it in sequence. A blend of the two is also perfectly fine; it's your choice. Read whatever you feel compelled to read, as this is what your subconscious mind is drawing you to.

The contents of the book were written to appeal to readers with an interest in dreams and beyond. Mysticism, science, the paranormal, metaphysics, shamanism, myth, storytelling, spirituality, folklore: all of these themes are explored in the pages.

You will find questions and exercises to help you examine your dreams even further, many of which can be expanded and used repeatedly at different times along your path of self-discovery. Practices such as journeying into your dreams, imagined with guided meditations, are designed to increase the expansion of your dream awareness and dream recall. Each chapter offers a way to look at dreams and discover how you can become the ultimate dreamer.

I recommend you use a journal to record your dreams. It's an essential tool if you want to be a serious dreamer, and there are suggestions on how to record your dreams. Your dreams are unique to you because you are unique in the world – this reality, at the very least. It follows then that interpretations of your dreams are personal, that your symbols and mythical motifs are yours alone. I have listed a number of generic dream meanings and questions to stimulate possibilities, but ultimately the understanding lies with you.

The following is a summary of the contents of each chapter.

Chapter 1
Dream essentials: all you need to know about dreams

To help you understand dream basics Chapter 1 takes you through the history, science and metaphysics of dreaming with some fundamental dream symbol interpretations. If you are new to the world of dreams then beginning with this chapter might be a good approach. Just know that we all dream, whether or not we remember our dreams.

Chapter 2
The collective dream directory

In general there are around 12 major universal dreams with some variations, but essentially dreams have basic common themes running through them. Whether you dream of losing your teeth or being chased, Chapter 2 contains the collective dream dictionary to explain the kind of dreams you wake up and think, 'That was a weird dream!'

Chapter 3
Dreaming during a worldwide pandemic

This chapter covers COVID-19 pandemic dreams from a world study of dreaming and my own research and experiences. I had several confusing, disturbing and prophetic dreams but, overall, they were in sync with the dream themes of many other people. Who knew we had the same dream imagery?

Chapter 4
Living your story through synchronicity and dreams

Living your life story being informed by your dreams can reap rewards for your well-being. Synchronicities, dreams, daydreams, serendipity and coincidences are not random; they are insights, information, knowledge, wisdom and truths presented to you as signs and exist to demonstrate there is more to you than you are aware of.

Chapter 5
The hero's journey

I've always had an interest in archetypal literature and movies, from my earliest books on fairy tales to blockbuster hero movies such as *Star Wars*. I was greatly influenced by Clarissa Pinkola Estés' classic *Women Who Run with the Wolves*. As a female I struggled to find a hero I could relate to who wasn't action packed and male driven, but I learned in time that a hero has many faces. Chapter 5 explores Joseph Campbell's *The Hero's Journey* myth and your own journey, in which you star as the hero of your life movie.

Chapter 6
Lucid dreaming

Lucid dreams are exceptional and vivid and make you want to dive into bed each night and prepare for the trip of a lifetime. Some people are natural lucid dreamers, awake in their dreams, while others have to learn how to get into this state. Chapter 6 takes you into the world of lucid dreaming, of out-of-body experiences, and teaches you practices that open up your potential to astral travel as the awakened dreamer.

Chapter 7
Shamanic dreaming

The earth-based wisdom of indigenous cultures has been ignored for far too long, but fortunately there is now a burgeoning interest in returning to native ways to heal the earth. Dreams in indigenous cultures were considered to be no different to reality. Chapter 7 takes you on a learning journey to shamanic trances where the shaman enters the dream world to find lost parts of your soul – which you will also learn how to do.

Chapter 8
Dreaming in multiple dimensions

By the time you reach Chapter 8 you will have acquired some very powerful dreaming knowledge that you can put into practice. This chapter, which will stretch your mind even further, is an intoxicating mix of quantum physics, metaphysics and spirituality: the big three! Parallel universes, the entanglement theory, past lives, Akashic records and the Mandela effect are all topics requiring a big leap to open your mind to the notion that dreams are much bigger than you may have originally thought.

Dreams offer an access point into the deeper parts of your higher self, known as the super conscious. Everything you need to know is within you; once you've finished reading you will never again say 'It's just a dream!' This book is a journey into your inner self and healing through your dream images as you action them in your waking life.

May you enjoy becoming an awakened dreamer as much as I will enjoy taking you on this journey.

MINDMAP
YOUR
DREAMS.

Chapter 1

DREAM ESSENTIALS: ALL YOU NEED TO KNOW ABOUT DREAMS

'A single dream is more powerful than a thousand realities.'

– J.R.R. TOLKIEN

As we spend a third of our lives in a sleep state during which we experience a surreal world of self-exploration, it's odd to hear people say dismissively 'It's just a dream'. Yet some people do consider dreaming time to be insignificant and only a part of the imaginative mind, not for a moment giving dreams the value they truly deserve. Whether it's a vivid dream or a nightmare teeming with significant images and emotions, they are easily banished as scenes belonging to fantasies and we often forget them by the time we've had breakfast. Few of us write down our dreams on waking.

This chapter will introduce you to dreams – not as symbols that are encrypted with a secret language created by your dreaming mind, but as an altered state of consciousness with deep insights that can assist you in your waking life.

THE STUDY OF DREAMS

We all dream. We may not remember them, but we all do dream. In fact, dreaming has both fascinated and baffled philosophers and scientists for thousands of years, and trying to understand the nature of dreams is not a new phenomenon. In ancient cultures dreams were thought to be some kind of supernatural communication or messages from the gods; sacred knowledge given as gifts from the dimensions beyond living reality.

Around 2,000 BCE in ancient Egypt dream temples were built in which the priests and priestesses interpreted dream visions. There was even a dream interpretation book in hieroglyphics. In later years the ancient Greeks worshipped at the dream temple of Asclepius (also known as Asklepius or Asklepios), where healing took place.

It was the duty of Roman citizens to report dreams that threatened the safety of the empire, so the professional diviner Artemidorus from the second century CE, the first real dream researcher, analysed and interpreted the dreams of the Roman Empire.

Indigenous cultures worldwide have regarded dreams as essential to the well-being of their people, as they believed they were messages from the ancestors, sacred guides and totem animals. The Dreamtime of the native Australian Aboriginal culture came from their ancestors, each tribe identifying with their own dream totem that was recognised and claimed to be part of their spiritual identity.

It's only in relatively modern times that the study of dreams has been taken seriously, with the father of dream analysis, Sigmund Freud, the sleeping prophet Edgar Cayce and the mystical psychologist Carl Jung among others, arousing interest in the scientific community and almost forcing us to take dreaming more seriously. And indeed we have. This book is one of thousands that deal with the understanding and study of dreams. The scientific study of dreams is known as *oneirology*; if you are fascinated by the world of dreams you are an *oneironaut*, an intrepid explorer of the dream world.

Did the ancients get it right? When we dream are we receiving messages from the divine, or is it a movie your brain has created for you to watch and experience during sleep? Perhaps it's a combination of both. We are moving into a time when science and metaphysics are coming to similar conclusions about the mystery of dreaming.

WHAT HAPPENS WHEN YOU SLEEP?

When you sleep you are in an altered consciousness in both mind and body, with little sensory activity and inhibition of nearly all voluntary muscles. Interactions with our environment are reduced, which means when you are sleeping your body is essentially still and in a state that is close to being dead, except you're breathing and your brain is active, your heart is pumping and your mind is filled with movie-like images called 'dreams'.

More significantly, *you sleep for one third of your lifetime* – that's about 25 years if we take 75 years as a lifetime. Of those 25 sleep years you spend six years dreaming, or about two hours each night, and you experience five to 10 dreams. Animals also dream, so your pet could be seeing their own movie in their sleeping mind at the same time as you see yours.

WHY IS DREAMING SO FASCINATING?

There are many facets to dreaming, layers of meaning, symbols and unexplained phenomena that have us intrigued. It could be as simple as dreaming being your subconscious mind going over the day's events and creating scenarios based around things you've experienced in real life, or are you simply awake in a parallel universe? When you're dreaming and sleeping you could actually be transporting yourself to another dimension where everything is almost identical to your earthly reality. This idea about the nature of dreams is equally as valid as are dreams that connect you to your loved ones who have passed on, your ancestors, your spirit guides and other beings.

Dreams are a treasure trove of information on the most intriguing topic: you. They help you gain some understanding of what's really going on inside, what's bothering you and how to face your worst fears: insights that can guide you through turbulent and emotional times. Learning to interpret your dreams is a great starting point on the road to self-discovery.

Dreams are not against you: they're on your side. Even nightmares are a tool to greater self-awareness. Dreams and nightmares provide an opportunity to tap into your subconscious mind to solve problems without your annoying and limited waking conscious getting in the way.

Every dream is connected to your own reality. While your unconscious mind is busy dreaming in images and not making much sense, it is also processing any problems you're experiencing and trying to provide solutions. Once you understand your personal dream symbols you'll gain insight into finding strategies to cope with your real-life issues. Whether it's the death of a loved one, the end of a marriage, leaving a job, empty nesting or not achieving a goal, it is bound to have a huge effect on your psyche. Whatever is suppressed in your conscious life will be revisited in your dreams, so that grieving and acknowledging the loss will offer insight on how to cope.

Ever dreamed your car wouldn't start? It could have something to do with the state of your health. Emotional stress is a major cause of physical and psychological problems, and dreams about machines breaking down, injuries or lifts not working represent a body in need of healing.

Dreams are a rich source of insight into relationships. By interpreting the symbols and metaphors in your dreams you can identify issues and be open to new methods of enhancing healthy and loving relationships. Awareness of your needs can be subjugated due to society's expectations, parental programming, self-image and an idealised version of a perfect relationship.

In your busy waking life you can miss cues that will allow you to dig deeper into your authentic needs. The dreaming mind won't allow you to be so easily distracted; you will experience disturbing dreams that remind you that you have been neglecting some aspect of your life that is related to relationships. The symbols are important to note, as are your emotions during and after the dream. You might be trying to fix a damaged car, collect dead branches from a tree or rescue an abused animal. Consider aspects of your relationships that are in neglect or think about you as the dreamer needing to survive a strained relationship.

We really do get our best ideas in dreams. Famous authors such as Charles Dickens and Stephen King are renowned for creating plots, scenery and characters from their dreamscapes. Colours, textures, sounds and dialogue are much more enhanced in dreams and give a writer so much material to use in their stories.

THE STAGES OF SLEEP AND DREAMING

Science has been more closely monitoring sleeping and dreaming states the last 25 years to interpret sleep patterns and why we dream. There are four to five stages of sleep: from light to deep to deepest, which is rapid eye movement (REM) sleep when our brains are most active but our bodies are paralysed. It's fortunate we can't move or we'd all be wandering around at night acting out our dream stories! We use the same level brain waves in REM as we do when we are awake.

> The highly brain-active REM state, which occurs every 90 minutes, is when the most vivid and memorable dreams occur. On average we dream for about two hours a night during any of the sleep stages, and unless you write down your dream immediately upon waking you'll forget 90 per cent of it after 10 minutes. It's a good practice to keep a pen and paper next to your bed so you don't forget the dream and miss out on any message it has for you.

The sleep cycle (from light to deep to deepest sleep) repeats itself an average of four to five times per night but may repeat as many as seven times, and most people remember between five and seven dreams a night. Within each cycle there may be many dream themes, which can seem like separate dreams. It could be argued that people have upwards of 250 dreams a night! No wonder you may sometimes feel exhausted when you wake up in the morning, especially if you've had lucid dreams.

WHY DO YOU DREAM?

For me, dreaming is transformative and my true north, guiding me to understand what is going on in the world around me at a collective level as well as in my own personal micro world. Dreams open a path to self-exploration and gaining insight

Every dream is connected to my own reality and is drawn from my personal experiences.

Dreams provide a powerful way of improving emotions and relationships. Although we mostly experience negative dreams – fear and anxiety, followed by fear and sadness – the challenge is to be open to these negative emotions and explore what's beneath them in your day-to-day reality. While your unconscious mind races around with weird movie-like scenarios it's also working out solutions to any problems or issues you're facing, and because dreams are intuitive they're very useful when it comes to discovering your true emotions.

Although there are many theories about why we dream, no one knows for sure. Following are some possible explanations.

Stress release and brain dump: dream insights can guide you through turbulent and emotional times, serving as a means of cleansing and releasing negative emotions. During a typical day you hold back your feelings and repress your anger, so dreams help you to cope with daily stresses by dumping them on your sleeping subconscious mind, where you can process and sort out all the problems you've encountered in waking life. The conscious brain needs to rest and recharge through shutting down; your brain and body regenerate during REM sleep. At the most basic level, dreams help you gain some understanding of what's bothering you and how to face your worst fears.

Filtering new events: you need dreams to filter new or traumatic events happening in your life. If you encounter potent emotions such as grief, loss, trauma and abuse your brain can't always retrieve those feelings from your existing emotional files to process them. Dreams *will* process the emotions and, most importantly, store them so your brain can familiarise itself with and be able to access them in real life. The contents of the dreams mirror your life events and can be used to help you cope better with future emotional situations.

Problem solving: author John Steinbeck said: 'It's a common experience that a problem difficult at night is resolved in the morning after the committee of sleep has worked on it', which led to the modern-day version 'Sleep on it!'

Many a problem has been solved by dreams and consequently come into consciousness. While you sleep your mind doesn't switch off; it becomes active instead. With knowledge comes insight, allowing your dreams to offer information on what's bothering you in your waking life and provide ways of overcoming your fears. Once you work out the symbols, which we will explore later, you'll gain greater understanding of what's going on with you and gain insight into what you need to do or what approach you should take.

For good mental and physical health: dream experts have suggested the purpose of dreams is to maintain sleep, which is essential for physical and psychological health. Dreaming not only reduces stress, it also gives your busy conscious mind a chance to close down the hormones responsible for assisting attention and memory while your body recovers and regenerates itself for another day. Dreams also seem to be a biological necessity for sleep. Tests on people who were prevented from entering the dream state before they could dream were more easily irritated while awake and performed badly.

Dreaming to remember: when you dream you're consolidating information or experiences from your waking state, and you dream in order to remember those experiences. Remember when you were told to study before you went to bed because then you would have retained more information when you woke up? This is apparently a direct result of the brain storing information in memory while sleeping.

Trauma studies have shown that when people go to sleep soon after a traumatic experience they are more likely to remember and be haunted by that trauma. One way to prevent this is to keep people awake and distracted with other things for a few hours to prevent them from going straight to sleep and dumping their traumatic experience into their memory bank. This also applies to watching the news just before going to sleep, which can result in bad dreams or nightmares if the news is particularly upsetting or has triggered something such as an ordeal or fear from the past.

For inspiration and spiritual guidance: dreams are mentioned in ancient and religious books as being prophetic and essential for oracles and fortune telling. We continue to use dreams for inspiration, creativity and spiritual guidance. When great composers wrote their opus or creative geniuses conceived their works they often enlisted the help of the dreaming state.

The melody for the song 'Yesterday' came to Beatles legend Paul McCartney in a dream. He woke up and stumbled to the piano by his bedside to work out the chords and is reported to have said: 'I just fell out of bed, found out what key I had dreamed it in and I played it.' Mary Shelley wrote the best-selling novel *Frankenstein* after being inspired by a dream she had. Stephen King writes his novels based on his nightmares, as did author and poet Edgar Allan Poe. Other scientific, philosophical and musical genius discoveries claimed to be revealed in dreams include the following:

◎ Nobel Prize–winning chemist August Kekulé discovered the hexagonal benzene ring structure at a molecular level.

- Dmitri Mendeleev created the periodic table of elements in complete form the way it was presented in dream.

- Classical music composer Igor Stravinsky heard the music to the orchestral work 'Rite of Spring' in a dream.

- Surrealist artist Salvador Dali claimed he loved dreams and many masterpiece artworks came from scenes in dreams, such as the 1944 work 'Dream Caused by the Flight of a Bee Around a Pomegranate a Second before Awakening'.

WHY ARE DREAMS SO CONFUSING?

Dreaming is much more significant than simply being a release from an overworked brain. The files stored each day in your brain are reordered by the dreaming mind and random emotional associations are slotted into systems. Dreams are confusing as they're trying to create a sense of order and file away emotional associations in a systemised way. The problem is that you don't know how to read this dream-run system, the subconscious system that underlines your unconscious fears and desires. It is much more powerful than the conscious mind.

If you are open to understanding your dreams you can access your subconscious and use it for better understanding of yourself and your needs, wants and aspirations.

Dream research is a burgeoning and ongoing field of study; the following is what some past famous dream experts said about dreams.

Neurologist and psychologist Sigmund Freud (1856–1939) has been recognised as the father of dream analysis for the modern era. He used dreams to analyse people's personalities by accessing their unconscious, which rules our deepest urges and desires.

He considered dreams to be sexually based desires and dreams themselves as a form of wish fulfilment (something that is not really happening in ordinary life). For Freud, dreams were about recognising the hidden parts we try to avoid or repress.

Psychiatrist and psychoanalyst Carl Gustav Jung (1875–1961) was a pupil of Freud's who developed a different theory of the unconscious and of dreams. Jung saw the unconscious as a more spiritual aspect of the self and dreams as a means of understanding the subconscious mind. He was more interested in looking at the purpose of dreaming than the causes and coined the term 'individuation', in which dreams are a guide to making ourselves whole and provide solutions to the problems encountered in the ordinary life.

Jung's 'archetypes' or 'universal symbols' are reflected in dreams and are contained in a collective unconscious: a collection of images, experiences and ideas all humans share that come from the earliest experiences of our ancestors. Patients were encouraged to deal with their own unconscious material and record their dreams carefully, even to illustrate them with pictures or models in wax or clay.

Psychiatrist, psychoanalyst and psychotherapist Fritz Perls (1893– 1970), the founder of Gestalt therapy, believed that dreams contain the unwanted or rejected parts of a person, that everything in a dream – person, object and image – represented a particular aspect. Perls' theory was that each dream image is unique to the individual dreamer, unlike Jung, who was more about universal experiences.

DIFFERENT KINDS OF DREAMS

Dreams hold up a mirror to everyday attitudes and actions, sometimes in a surprising or funny way, and help you to see yourself from a new perspective. Russian novelist Fyodor Dostoevsky (1821–81) had this to say about different types of dreams and their purpose:

Dreams seem to be spurred on not by reason but by desire, not by the head but by the heart, and yet what complicated tricks my reason has played sometimes in dreams.

Compensatory dreams are about seeking to balance what is denied through healthy expression. Thoughts, viewpoints and feelings you experience in your waking life are secretly stored in the unconscious mind, eventually surfacing in your dreams. Perhaps you are normally a serious person who plays the role of a clown in your dream. It may be that a part of you feels unloved and in your dream you are surrounded by affection and comfort. You could live in a cramped city apartment with little ventilation and in the dream you're galloping through rolling hills in the countryside.

It is easy to become unbalanced in life and focus too much on one thing, and many of us are very good at wearing figurative masks when operating in working life. If you spend too much time on the masked part of yourself whereby you play a role the psyche rebels, which will result in dreams that pull your attention towards those things you've been neglecting or avoiding in order to create balance in the psyche. Not enough balance between work and family? A holiday is long overdue and you're avoiding taking time off because you think you're indispensable? You could end up having a compensatory dream that forces you to adopt a more middle-ground approach to life.

Wish fulfilment dreams express hidden literal or symbolic wishes, or see you trying on possible futures. What would it be like to be rich and famous when you are scraping by with the most basic lifestyle? What would it be like to win a Nobel Prize for medicine? It's fantasy but a useful fantasy in that you are able to recognise what it is your heart desires and perhaps find a way to realise it in waking life – or at least the emotion associated with it such as popularity, acceptance, esteem or desirability.

Precognitive dreaming is not working out future events from an existing situation but is rather dreaming something before it happens, such as riots, wars and natural catastrophes. This can also apply to personal events.

Creative dreams inspire inventions and masterpieces. The hypnagogic state, or the transitional period between wakefulness and sleeping (see also further on in this chapter), is where the genius or visionary muses reveal themselves. Will you give the muse a chance in your dream to reveal your next masterpiece?

Archetypal or collective dreams relate mostly to working out questions that are universal; it's not all about you. These dreams deal with patterns of behaviour or belief systems that are universally shared. Archetypes are universal dreams, experiences, images, patterns and symbols that reside within us all. They represent models of universal behaviours or personality traits. They emerge in symbolic form in dreams, mythology, fairy tales and ancient traditions. Some common archetype characters we see in dreams are the divine child or inner child, the great mother, the wise old man or woman, the trickster, the princess or damsel in distress and the hero and heroine.

They are known as 'big dreams' and have a clear message to the psyche. These significant dreams are often vivid and can be strange and confusing. To understand them you need to know the mythological background and the symbols and motifs of different cultures at different times. Unconsciously we still think as our distant ancestors did, and to recognise this is to deepen your experience and open up new possibilities.

A collective dream will present 'archetypes' from the 'collective unconscious' and have special meaning for others as well as the dreamer. Our shared dream experiences serve to connect us as a human race. In times of crisis, our dreams and unite us.

Warning dreams: occasionally dreams seem to be clear warnings of danger. If you dream of falling off a ladder, crashing your car, your house catching on fire or you are falling off a cliff, do take the dream seriously. You may have missed cues from your subconscious mind that the car brakes were not depressing hard enough or the heater was making a strange clicking noise, that you are in danger from something happening, and this is manifested in your dreams. Note that, however, dreaming of death does not necessarily indicate a fatal accident; there could be either a symbolic death or an actual physical death.

Numinous dreams: numinous dreams are strongly religious or spiritual. Ancient cultures were aware that dreams gave access to sources of wisdom beyond the ordinary, offering glimpses into the future and providing possible alternatives.

Parapsychological dreams include the telepathic, afterlife, past or future life, meeting guides, angels or dead ancestors, parallel lives and all phenomena that can't be easily explained.

Hypnagogic dreams: if you find you can't remember your dreams you can explore the borderland sleep state, known as the liminal space or threshold. It is an altered state of consciousness between being awake and asleep, a sacred space that takes place in a four-dimensional state in which your senses are highly attuned to the spiritual world.

Shamanic dreams involve elements of initiation, ritual, healing for others and guidance and are passed down from shamanic traditions by indigenous cultures. If we lose contact with our dreams the North American Iroquois believe we lose a vital part of our souls. Indigenous communities worldwide regard dreaming as an essential part of living a fully awakened life.

Healing dreams: metaphysics is a branch of philosophy that concerns abstract concepts such as being, knowing, identity, time and space. Metaphysicists believe the body receives images as physical events (what you should do or look for in response to physical ailments) and responds accordingly. For example, if you dream you are digging a garden and you come across a disfigured tree root it may mean you have an illness or condition that needs to be addressed and is related to an abnormality. Images that persuade the body to self-heal are delivered to you through your dreams, while emotional healing dreams put you in touch with multiple aspects of yourself including the shadow side you may have repressed or denied.

Lucid dreams: in a lucid dream you're aware you're dreaming while you're dreaming. In some cases you can direct the events and outcome of the dream, that is, you can manipulate the dream and make it go in whatever direction you want.

Dream sharing: one curious feature of dreaming is the way that close friends or members of the same family, particularly a husband and wife or parents and children, dream the same dream without previously having related it to each other. Still more curious is the way children dream about their parents' problems even if these have been carefully hidden from them. The dream will not usually be a straightforward statement but will be symbolic and often picturesque.

Recurring dreams are dreams that repeat themselves. Sometimes they are exactly the same each time they are dreamed; other times the emotion will be the same but the details or ending will change. For example, you are being chased by an aggressive figure and always end up in the same place you can't escape from. You want to get out of the situation but you know it's going to end the same way. At this point you wake up feeling fearful, angry, annoyed and frustrated, or other negative feelings that have come to the surface. Recurring dreams can also be humorous and you're not too concerned about the inevitable ending.

Recurring dreams indicate a real-life issue that hasn't been confronted or resolved so your anxiety forces you to keep dreaming about it. These dreams call your attention to something you need to change, and will repeat until you acknowledge the problem and resolve the issue. Check with your daily diary to see what anniversary, event or emotion could have triggered the recurring dream and work to deal with it. When you do so, the recurring dream will stop.

Nightmares: nightmares can be experienced by both children and adults. They are vividly realistic and disturbing, will often awaken us and leave us feeling terrified. They may be caused by a number of factors such as watching a scary movie or the news before bed time, late-night snacks, certain medications such as anti-depressants and narcotics, sleep deprivation and psychological triggers such as anxiety and post-traumatic stress disorder. At the heart of nightmares is a fear of not surviving.

FORGETTING YOUR DREAMS

If you find you can't remember your dreams you're not alone: most of us forget our dreams on waking. Many people declare they never dream, but everybody has several dreams per night. As most dreams occur at the end of the sleeping cycle (REM sleep) and are often interrupted by having to get up in a hurry in the morning, there is no time for your brain to take a moment to recall the dream vividly unless it has had an emotional impact on you.

TIPS FOR REMEMBERING YOUR DREAMS

There are many physiological and psychological reasons for forgetting your dreams, but the most important thing is to consider whether or not you have consciously stopped dreaming your inner dreams, your passions. When there's a drought in your vision there will be a greater chance that you forget your dreams. Dreams need to be mined like gold or silver or diamonds; their value lies in their uniqueness to you. Dreams are the secret wishes of your soul, the connection to your deepest intuition.

Try these tips and see how your dreamwork progresses.

Intention. Before going to bed, set the intention to remember your dreams. You may want to re-read some of your previous dreams in your dream diary to strengthen the waking to dreaming bridge, or meditate on a question you'd like answered. Everybody dreams, so if you can't remember your dreams set your intention before going to bed. Ask for a dream.

> *Tip:* write the intention down and put it under your pillow. Use lavender oil to awaken your memory sense and make sure you are relaxed before going to sleep. Use meditation techniques, music or guided meditation. You also can find a number of apps to help you with going to sleep.

Keep a dream journal. Write down the dream as soon as you wake up, using as many details as possible including the date. Most importantly, list all the emotions you felt during the dream. Within five minutes of waking up you lose 50 per cent recollection of what you dreamed and, after 18 minutes, 90 per cent of the recollection will be gone. Occasionally if the dream is a vivid one you will carry a part of it with you for the day, but most of the smaller details will have been forgotten. Record your dreams daily.

> *Tip:* keep a blank journal by your bed and write down everything you remember. As you keep a journal over the years you'll notice the rhymes and loops or cycles in your life. Dreams are like looking after a garden: they will bloom and thrive if you pay attention and tend them regularly.

Sketch or draw if it helps you to record your dreams. The dream you recall the most will be the last one you had before you woke up; if you remember just a fragment, try not to judge or interpret it. You will have a series of dreams – some people remember up to 10 dreams per night – but you may consider the fragments incomplete and unimportant. Every part of the dreamscape is essential, with many gold nuggets being found in the fragments.

If you remember your dreams, start with them. If you don't, start with whatever thoughts and feelings are with you as you welcome the new day or in that interval between two sleeps (the sleep-wake state),when creative ideas, precognitive visions and spiritual awakenings often stream through.

Keep your eyes closed. Keep your eyes closed and remain in your waking position. The dream can easily be dislodged, especially if you are thinking of your day's schedule. Stay present with the dream, like you are holding a precious young baby. Be gentle with your waking self and beware of the sudden jolt between being in deep sleep and fully awake. That abrupt severing could cause you to lose the elusive dream, which will flit and fly away if you don't gently encourage it to remain with you.

> *Tip:* avoid using an alarm clock. Train your body to wake you up instead; you'll be amazed by how accurate your body clock can be.

Connect common images to specific situations in your waking life. Ask yourself: does the theme remind you of anything or anyone in your life? What's been going on in the last few days or weeks? What event or emotion may have triggered the dream? What emotions were felt during the dream and when you woke up? With regular use of your dream journal you will find you can create your own personal dictionary of symbols.

When you analyse your dream it helps to identify how you feel. Once these emotions are brought to the surface you can deal with the issues related to them if you choose.

> *Tip:* keep twin journals: a journal of the day and a journal of the night. In the night journal record your dreams, and in the day journal track signs and synchronicities you see in your daily life so you can open up to awareness of the world around you.

Persistence. As with any area in which you want to succeed, you have to persevere with the activity until it becomes part of your routine. The more you engage with the world of dreams the richer your connection with your inner self will be. Make it a priority to read books on dreams, share dreams with friends and family, keep a dream journal and incubate dreams when you need guidance.

Don't neglect your dream world. Deepen your practice for long enough and you will consider your dream journey the most essential history of your inner life. Recording dreams will allow you to get in touch with your inner wisdom and assist you in using your intuition to make decisions about your waking life.

INTERPRETING DREAMS

Every dreamer's dream has a personal meaning. A dream dictionary can shine some light on probable interpretations, but ultimately you have to intuitively work out what your dreams mean to you. It will depend on your background, circumstances and emotional state and the issues you are facing in your waking world. No two people will have the exact same issues and life circumstances, therefore dream symbols will vary from person to person.

No matter what nationality, gender or social status we have, our dreams have common, universal themes and sequences. Jung called it the *collective unconscious*; that is, we are linked intuitively and we share emotional states through dreaming. Following are some methods of undertaking your own dream interpretation. Remember: it's your dream and it is unique to you.

- ◎ **Describe the dream.** Write down in as much detail as possible all the elements of your dream. Particularly note the settings, people and animals, objects, feelings and actions in the dream.

- ◎ **Relate the dream to someone or retell it to yourself.** Edit the dream a little to bring out the main theme. The words you use may trigger the meaning and theme of the image. Give the dream a book title if you think it will help. Look at the emotions in the dream and compare those feeling to how you are feeling in everyday life.

- ◎ **Make connections to real-life images or situations.** Does the theme remind you of anything or anyone in your life, or does it remind you of any part of yourself? Read the dreams of the past week two or three times to consolidate the lessons or insights.

- ◎ **Ask each dream image questions.** For example, ask a car why it is driving so fast and recklessly; or ask a house what it is doing in the middle of the forest; or ask water why it is trying to drown you? See what each part of the dream tells you.

◎ **If it were my dream ...** This technique involves telling your dreams to friends so they can interpret it by saying: 'If it were my dream I'd be asking why I drove faster than usual in the bomb of a car when I have a really good car in real life.' Having other people own your dream will give you some new insights you hadn't considered.

◎ **Practice interpreting your dreams to increase your understanding.** Make up a little codebook for yourself. For example, every time I move house I dream of a dragon, or when I dream of a snake I usually meet up with someone from the past I don't like. Only your subconscious knows what your dreams mean to you.

WHAT ARE YOUR DREAMS TELLING YOU?

Following are some of the most common life themes to show up in the dream world.

RELATIONSHIPS

Dreams shine a light on how you interact with those around you, problems with relationships and ways to enhance and promoting loving and healthy relationships. Dreams may ask you to:

◎ be aware of your interactions with those around you

◎ face issues of intimacy and loss

◎ identify negative or confusing emotions connected with relationships

◎ analyse sexual and infidelity issues.

SELF-ESTEEM

Not smart enough, not attractive enough, not good enough . . . Dreams will shine the light on issues around self-esteem and self-development. You may discover dream symbols that will ask you to:

- find ways of deeply appreciating and accepting yourself
- identify negative habits and self-beliefs that are no longer needed
- implement new strategies in your life to make yourself feel good.

GRIEF AND LOSS

Whether it's the death of a loved one or the 'death' of a marriage, job or personal wish, any ending will have a huge effect on your psyche. Whatever is suppressed in your conscious life will be re-enacted in your dreams. These sad and often confusing dreams may come up from your subconscious to acknowledge the loss you are experiencing and offer insight into how to:

- resolve painful memories and find greater peace
- gain insight into what's causing you to grieve
- connect to your intuitive self
- help you understand the message in your dream, which will give you strategies to cope.

HEALTH AND BODY

Emotional stress is a major cause of physical and psychological illness. Your stress will be highlighted and exaggerated through anxiety dreams and nightmares, making you more aware of physical and emotional symptoms that need to be addressed in waking life so you can reprogram your behavioural responses to improve your life. Your dreams may be gently communicating to you so you will be empowered to:

- identify symbols telling you to seek medical help
- explore healing on an emotional level
- confront recurring dreams
- understand dreams as a gateway to your subconscious.

Note that your dreams can be affected by medication that will cause you to experience disturbing and frightening dreams that will make you fearful about falling asleep. It's important you understand that the disturbing dreams are one of the side effects of taking the medication and you shouldn't be too concerned, but do discuss it with your GP if you are overly worried.

I HAVE
THE
POWER
TO DREAM
AND DO.

Chapter 2

THE COLLECTIVE DREAM DIRECTORY

'A dream is a microscope through which we look at the hidden occurrences in our soul.'

– ERICH FROMM

The study of dreams is not an exact science, and no one is better equipped than the dreamer to truly make sense of a dream's meaning and messages. The directory in this chapter breaks down the most common dreams into a simple structure where you, the dreamer, can begin the mystical journey into your deepest self and make sense of your inner world. Once you get a glimpse of your innermost or subconscious self you can begin to make sense of your outer world.

This dream directory is designed for you to understand the main elements of universal dream themes, the dreams we all share collectively regardless of culture, ethnicity, religion or gender. It is normal for us to share humanity's fears and anxieties and fight for survival, and over the years through my books, seminars and personal appearances I have helped people understand their dreams as part of their journey into self-actualisation.

Some dream scenarios might present themselves as recurring dreams or nightmares or seem nonsensical. If you take the time to understand your dream patterns and symbols and work out possible dream meanings you will be able to follow suggested actions. Your dream may be validating your waking decisions, or it may be prodding you to make more informed decisions. Even when you have weird dreams that don't seem as though they belong to you, you can ask yourself what pieces of disparate information are creating a plan for you.

There is no down side to working through your dreams, no matter how trivial the content might be. Dreams guide us and give us valuable insights into our psyche – why and how we respond to the world and people around us.

To really get to the heart of a dream you need to break it down.

Action: what is happening; what events led up to the dream?

Characters: who is in the dream?

Location: where are you?

Emotions: how do you personally and your body feel?

Perspective is important in a dream. Who are you: the star or the observer? If you are the star, which happens mostly in nightmares or highly anxious dreams where you are playing yourself, it indicates you have a fixed identity; it is happening to you. At other times you may be the third person witnessing the dream, which can make you feel less threatened but you will also miss out on the experience as you are removed from the scene.

> By delving into your dreams you create a road map to finding yourself and your soul's desires and a glimpse of an alternate future. When you bring back the wisdom from your dreamscape you bring new life in your waking world and leave behind parts of your fragmented self.

As a dream researcher and vivid dreamer I know that dreams change in shape and nature according to personal circumstances and what's going on for the global community. It's most effective to regard dreams as movies and you as being the actor playing many parts: sometimes the main star and other times an extra. You may even be sitting in the theatre simply watching. This will help you to make the most out of the experience and be able to bring back the lessons from the dream world.

The previous chapter presented a framework to build on with deeper knowledge and practices. This chapter is a practical approach to dreams and offers you the opportunity to work with the most common dreams we all experience. Activities and exercises are provided as a guide for you to follow.

PEOPLE YOU MEET

Taking the point about being in a movie, people in dreams are characters who play a part in order for you to understand something. The people you see in your dreams are an aspect of your relationships to others and to yourself. What does that person represent to you? What qualities does the person have that you may need right now? Ask the people in your dreams who they are and what they want, which will reflect aspects of yourself.

An **old man or woman** is associated with wisdom, with elders who have lived a full life and can pass on their knowledge and experience. What gifts do these elders bring? Are you in need of guidance?

We tend to dream of an old wise man or woman when we need to be pointed in the right direction. Dreaming of elderly relatives – either living or departed – represents a quality you normally associate with them. Take note: it could be they are telling you to embrace ageing or to grow up.

Parents and authority figures represent power due to their status. What qualities do these figures possess that can be used in your current situation? When you dream of meeting authority figures such as police, bosses, teachers or law enforcement agents you are either rejecting their authority (breaking some rule) or feeling intimidated by them. If you are feeling disempowered, consider how you can change that negative emotion.

Mothers are connected to your nurturing self. Are you in need of nurturing, or are you not giving nurture to others? A father figure offers protection and good standards of behaviour and guidance. The negative side of the father figure is as a strict disciplinarian who aims to repress individuality.

A **baby** dream suggests there is something new coming your way: a fresh phase, a new relationship or project. It's important that you take good care of this new life as it is fragile and vulnerable. If the baby is helpless, upset or unwell it's time to give your relationship some attention and priority over a new project, whether it's a different career or lifestyle change.

Dreaming of a young child you don't recognise is likely to be your own inner child. What are they asking you to do? Perhaps have more fun and find more joy in life? Or maybe you grew up too soon through no fault of your own and it's time to accept that part of your past. I know a number of dreamers whose childhood was denied to them for a number of reasons. The term 'parentification' refers to children who had to take on the parental role and responsibilities very early on.

Pregnancy and being pregnant is a common symbol for creativity, so in a sense it's talking about a new life. Are you patiently waiting for a fresh part of your life to begin? It may be that you are losing hope because nothing seems to be working out as you had imagined in your timeframe. Remember that it takes nine months for gestation and in that time you prepare for the new arrival. It's wise to prepare and gain confidence during this period of waiting so when the change arrives it won't cause too much upheaval.

To dream of being pregnant is to be filled with new beginnings and potential. It's definitely a dream about change. For some women who have dreamed of being pregnant it has actually eventuated, but although this is not common you shouldn't be surprised that your subconscious mind picks up messages from your body much earlier than you would consciously.

If you see a pregnant woman in your dream, ask yourself 'Why am I having this dream now?' Dreams have a knack of showing up when you most need to heed their message.

A **cheating partner** dream can be very upsetting, as one of the more painful dreams is that of betrayal. These dreams are very common because as couples we dread this scenario, and the media churns out infidelity scandals relentlessly. How can you ever be sure you will never be cheated on?

If you are feeling visibly jealous or enraged in your dream, what is it about the other man or woman that affects you the most? Notice if they are more attractive than you or they are someone familiar. What parts of yourself have you not shared with your partner? Do you feel your partner is attracted to certain qualities in others that you don't possess? It's time to do some shadow work and look at all parts of yourself that you've disowned or repressed.

Emotions can extend from jealously to being appalled, frightened and betrayed. When you wake up you know it's just your deepest fears that are at play, except that you carry this distrust into your ordinary life. If you have no basis for distrust you need to look deeper into yourself to find out where these insecurities are coming from or what triggered them.

If you are the unfaithful partner and in your dream it was the most exciting affair you could ever have desired, it may be that your lover had qualities you wanted to embody. You may be looking for a more physical or emotional connection. Was it someone you know – a work colleague, ex-lover or celebrity – or was it a stranger or the least likely friend or person you would ever want to be sexually involved with? Think about traits you lack or want to improve on. The dream might also be suggesting you look at ways to refresh your relationship and bring more courtship back into your lives.

Dreaming of **cheating with your ex** suggests your subconscious is warning you of repeating old habits from your failed relationship or recapturing the best of those past experiences with a view to integrating them into your present or future relationship. If you're a woman you may be searching for your animus (your masculine aspect), or if you're a man your anima (your feminine side) so that you can integrate yourself into wholeness.

Ghost dreams are universally experienced. Stories about ghosts terrify children at the same time as they enthral them. Some Asian cultures believe that if the deceased are not given a proper burial they will turn into ghosts that forever haunt and roam the world. They are known as 'hungry ghosts'.

If you dream about ghosts, ask yourself what's haunting you about your past. It may be ambitions not fulfilled, expectations not met or old memories best forgotten but still grieved about. What haven't you given a proper burial to, let go of and moved on from? Are there parts of you that are like the ghost you saw in the dream, parts of you that you haven't owned or have hidden away?

If someone you know who died a long time ago appears in your dream you may wonder why is it you can talk to them as if they were alive when you know they are dead. You might wake up distressed and confused, but know that this is part of the grieving process. Try to feel joyful that you've spent time with them even though they've passed on.

Ghosting is a fairly recent term that describes the practice of suddenly ending all contact with a person without explanation, particularly when in a relationship. If you are a victim of ghosting or you've been ghosted the suddenness of being cut off without any rhyme or reason can be a devastating blow to your self-esteem. You are made to feel that your relationship was not even worth the effort of a polite exit. Maybe the confrontation was too difficult for your partner or not worth the trouble, but that doesn't make it any easier for you.

Ghosts in this context are showing parts of your life that need closure.

An **intruder** breaking in to your home or car, a terrorist holding you up for ransom or threatening to kill you or an attacker hijacking you on your way home all form part of feeling threatened and, as such, represent your anxieties in your waking life. Ask yourself what triggered the dream: does it remind you of the fear or anxiety you experienced? Who or what is a threat to you? Do you have good boundaries, or do you allow people to zap you of time and energy?

If security is a big fear for you, what is making you feel unprotected, exposed and vulnerable in your ordinary life? It may be as simple as you needing to set boundaries or as complex as post-traumatic stress. Tune in to the emotions in your dream for some insight, as it may be telling you that you have untapped courage and strength.

HOUSES, ROOMS AND BUILDINGS

The setting of your dreams provides a backdrop for the scene and will often help you to link the aspects of your waking life the dream relates to. Ask yourself where you belong and feel safe.

Dreams about a **house** symbolise a larger aspect of your *self*, and how you feel about yourself and your life. Each room symbolises a different aspect of yourself and your life.

An **empty house** may be telling you something about your personal life: are you lonely? Does anyone want to live there? Maybe an unknown part of your life is coming up as an empty house in your dream. Look for clues in the dream scenery by the way each room makes you feel, then see what each room means below.

If the house is neglected, what does that say about what's going on in your life? Understand you need to pay more attention to yourself and take responsibility for it. What makes a house a home? Do you feel at home with yourself and with your environment? Take note of all the images in the dream, as they each have a story to tell and a message to bring to your conscious mind.

The **childhood home** is where it all began and your dreams will often place you there. Dreaming of your childhood home might be a way of revisiting emotional issues in your waking life that deal with family-based beliefs from that time. It could indicate you are repeating the same mistakes from your past and it's time to change this childhood conditioning and belief patterns.

The **ground floor** represents daily routine and what's currently going on in your waking life. Are you stuck somewhere on the ground floor? It may be time to move from this safe but predictable place.

A **hallway** in a dream shows that you have reached an area that is necessary to travel through so you can get to the other side. It's a bridge or a threshold. If you see closed doors on either side you may need to open them so you can expand your awareness to more possibilities. Is your life on pause? Are you still making your way through potential possibilities when you need to be making decision?

Empty rooms and discovering **new rooms** in a house reflect the rediscovery of lost aspects of yourself. As you wander through empty rooms and undiscovered wings of a familiar house, ask yourself if your life feels empty or incomplete. Is there something more but you don't know what? Are you half finishing things? When you search through empty rooms or discover new parts of the house it suggests your creativity needs expressing and that, like the new rooms, you need to rediscover parts of yourself you've neglected or put on hold.

Attics or roof space storage are where you keep memorabilia and unused or discarded items. It's the highest room in the house and symbolises the mind, that part of your body that is closest to the spiritual world. It may suggest you are ready for more self-awareness or a spiritual awakening. Look at how you are feeling in the dream: if you are nostalgic or pensive it may be that you are storing memories even though they are they still present in your mind. Old clothing or old-fashioned items might suggest looking for old aspects of yourself or a yearning to go back to the way things were. Ask yourself what's holding you back from moving forward.

Basements and cellars or spaces under the house are representative of your subconscious mind and all that is kept hidden or not expressed. This part of yourself deals with habits, ego, fears, old belief systems and conditioning that are ignored and hidden away. What are your greatest fears you have to keep a lid on? Why aren't you exploring this dark subterranean part of yourself? Shining a light might just illuminate those things that need recognition, healing or acceptance.

The **kitchen** is where you are nurtured and is a place to socialise with your family or friends. It is the best place in the house when you need comfort and nourishment, and also a place where you can be creative with cooking dishes.

The social aspect of the kitchen is highlighted in your dream. Is your social life in turmoil? Do you need more nourishment? What about your creativity: are you feeling uninspired and that your life is mundane humdrum?

The **living or family room** is closely related to the kitchen and represents your daily interactions with other people. Which people in your dreams are in your living room, and what do they represent to you? Think about what aspect of yourself they symbolise. If the room is bare, maybe you need to think about reaching out to others; if the room is crowded with too many people or is being trashed, you need to set new boundaries.

The **bathroom and toilet** are the most private rooms in the house where you take care of your physical body, cleansing and pampering yourself. It's also where you release and dispose of your bodily functions. If the bathroom or toilet is not functioning, you can't find it or there is no privacy, it suggests you are finding it difficult to express your needs in real life. On a practical note, it could also be your physical body warning you that you need to wake up and go to the bathroom.

Bedrooms represent the unconscious mind, resting, sleeping, privacy, intimacy and, of course, dreaming. If you observe yourself sleeping in your bedroom in your dream you may be experiencing lucid dreaming or be remembering to focus on an aspect of your life represented by this most private room.

Buildings are connected to the self but not as directly as are individual rooms. If you see buildings in your dreams you might be surprised to note a direct correlation to how you are feeling about your inner environment.

A **castle** is not just about its grandeur, but more often about feeling protected. What do you need to defend yourself against?

A **church or religious building** might be a call to develop your spiritual life or simply a need to retreat.

Public buildings suggests work relationships need more effort, while a **factory** is more about you feeling that life is a grind and you are a cog in the wheel.

A **hotel** is a common dream image representing something that is temporary in your life. It's a stepping stone, or else you are perched somewhere for just a while until something more permanent comes your way. It can also be that you feel like a stranger or a tourist, you don't belong. Do you feel ungrounded and need to set down roots? Perhaps you feel you need to escape from the traditional suburban existence and travel to exciting places.

LANDSCAPES

Landscapes and places in your dreams mirror your own internal landscape. Are you comfortable at home and at work? If you are then you are comfortable inside yourself, but an unfamiliar environment or one that is full of hazard and obstacles indicates you may be experiencing some inner struggle. The setting is an essential element of a dream as it provides the link between your dream-life adventures and your waking life. Ask yourself these questions about your waking life: Where am I? Where am I going to? What path do I follow? What am I looking for?

Deserts are dry and lack water (emotions, feeling, creativity), and suggest some parts of yourself you have neglected. What haven't you been paying attention to that needs nurturing?

The vastness of **oceans** represents the depths of your psyche. We are all but drops of water in an ocean; however, a drop of water from the ocean contains the same chemical structure and similar properties as the entire ocean. Each of us is no less important in creating the ocean. Do you feel connected to your deepest self? Are you feeling disconnected to others?

Being lost in your dream reflects your waking life situation when you are at the beginning of a fresh chapter and nothing is familiar to you. You literally don't know your way around, and that makes you anxious. The busier the scene – such as being lost in a large city, a multi-level car park, a dense forest or a high-rise building – the more anxious you are likely to feel in your dream. Ask yourself if you are feeling disconnected from yourself or in a new situation, and what it would take for you to feel comfortable.

Crossroads in myths and folktales are magical places between worlds where you can communicate with supernatural spirits and the elementals of the fairy world. You may be experiencing a crisis in your life, avoiding making choices and feeling bogged down with indecision. The dream is reaching out to you to be brave and make a move that will connect you to a path that will take you to a resolution.

Dark underground places such as car parks, tunnels, caves, subways and mines are symbols of the unconscious; it is in those places that lie the deepest, darkest, emotions that are kept hidden from your conscious mind. They are not places you want to explore as they are unknown and dangerous and far from your comfort zone. However, you need to explore this hidden terrain so you can reach an understanding of those parts of yourself that are rarely brought to the surface.

Underground is also the place to be when you don't want to be found. Are you escaping from a situation, person, decision or relationship? You may need to retreat for a while to regain your sense of purpose. At least once in your lifetime you will experience the dark night of the soul where you turn inwards and sit with your darkest thoughts.

Mines are notorious for toxic air and dangerous working conditions. Consider whether you are surrounded by toxic people or, indeed, you are not clearing out your emotions. It may be time to clean your environment, physically and metaphorically. Mines also have precious metals, gems and crystals: it's only when you mine deep that you bring back precious awakenings.

The **workplace** is where you spend a significant amount of time, so it will come as no surprise that you often dream of your work environment. If you dream of a previous workplace but nobody in the dream recognises you, it could well mean you are no longer the same person. You've moved on, although there's a part of you that is nostalgic and wants to recapture the old camaraderie.

Dreaming of a present workplace and feeling anxious suggests your waking life is carrying over to your dreaming cycle. When do you switch off? Are you able to balance your lifestyle? Are you struggling to get on with your colleagues or boss?

Unknown landscapes can create anxiety. If you are in an unfamiliar landscape you may be feeling lost and abandoned in your day-time life. Perhaps you've lost parts of yourself and no longer recognise who you've become. The dream is asking you to communicate more clearly with those around you, to ask for help with directions or guidance rather than trying to figure it out solo.

TRAVEL

Travel by its very nature indicates movement from A to B. How you travel is therefore very significant in a dream.

Driving is the means by which we go from one place to another. It's a problem if the person in control of the car is not paying attention or is driving dangerously.

Cars are symbols of movement, direction and life changes and represent parts of your physical body along with your drive and ambition. Generally, a car represents your drive (the engine and accelerator) for success and direction in life (the steering wheel). It's important to note whether in your dream you are the driver or the passenger, whether you are in control of where you are going in life or you're simply going along for the ride and letting others control you.

A dream of a **car crash** represents an emotional problem that is out of control. If you are steering from the back seat, ask yourself what impossible situation you are facing at home or in your relationship.

Uphill climbs indicate you have challenges ahead.

Roadblocks suggest obstacles.

Intersections in a dream, similarly to crossroads in your waking life, show you that you have choices and upcoming decisions.

No brakes are a terrifying marker that you are out of control and in danger of burnout.

Do you have a **flat tyre**? That indicates something that will halt your progress and prevent you from moving forward. Flatness can also indicate your mental and physical state.

Difficulty seeing the road ahead, because the wipers or headlights don't work, suggests you are feeling uncertain about your future. Is your vision clear, or are there potential obstacles in the way of your future?

Luggage symbolises things that we take with us that we feel we need, even thought we don't need all of what is packed away. Are you carrying emotional baggage? Do you need to lighten your load so you can travel lightly on your life journey? The dream may be challenging you to leave excess luggage behind if you want to make progress.

Flying without being in an aircraft is a common characteristic of lucid dreaming in which you suddenly realise you are dreaming and you are able to fly because it's only a dream. It is a positive dream of exhilaration, feeling like there are infinite possibilities and freedom, and a wish fulfilment dream about escapism and flying high in the success stakes. You want to capture that excitement in your waking life. If you are a pilot in the dream it suggests you feel in control of your life and are able to spread your wings. If you are a passenger it most likely indicates you are not ready to commit to a new possibility of freedom.

Flying has also been associated with sexual release. Once tension is released the dreamer has the sensation of freedom, much the same way as you'd feel if you were flying.

Airports and terminals are places of transition. When you are travelling and all is going smoothly in your dream you can enjoy the scenery and be sociable, experiencing your real-life need for adventure and leaving the everyday worries behind. However, it's frustrating if you miss the train by a fraction of a second, can't find your passport or your baggage breaks open or is lost.

Ask yourself if you are well prepared to reach an important decision or if you are on track with your goals. How can you be more connected with your own dreams and desires and who can you call on to help?

Alien spacecraft dreams can reflect a need for escape, to experience adventure and learn more about the universe. If the dream experience is negative and there's abduction by aliens, you most likely feel powerless and lacking in control in your waking life. Who are the aliens in your life? Are you feeling alienated? If you interpret this as a numinous (religious or spiritual) dream, dreaming of aliens may indicate spiritual guidance or experience.

Bridges indicate transition, moving from one state to another, which can be dangerous as you are leaving the familiar to step into the unknown. How you feel in the dream is the key to your emotional landscape. What if you are on a rickety bridge? What if you don't know where the bridge leads to on the other side? What if you can't turn back? Take a leap of faith and jump into the next chapter of your life. Have the courage to face new challenges and make decisions not based on fear of moving in a new direction.

ANXIETY DREAMS

From being naked in public to your teeth falling out, this section unravels the mystery behind the most common anxiety dreams and nightmares. These often frightening dreams are bad dreams with the volume turned up loud: they exist to get your attention. Notice when they appear and what is going on in your waking life; it may be that you need to find a new emotional response.

Ask yourself these questions when you encounter these stressful situations in your dreamscape: why am I feeling so anxious? How do I make this stop? What qualities do I need to overcome these situations? What strategies should I implement?

Being **naked in public** is dream of emotional vulnerability and reflects the feeling that you are exposed for who you really are, that others can see through the masks you wear in your social or work persona. You'd struggle to find someone who hasn't had a dream in which they're naked in full view of onlookers, as it is the number one most feared and embarrassing situation.

Naked dreams will come up at various stages of your life, often when you're starting a new phase in your life such as a job or relationship or you are about to move or travel. Anxiety and lack of confidence are two main triggers for this dream: you may have a fear of being scrutinised or ridiculed for revealing who you really are. Where in life are you feeling unskilled and lacking in confidence? On the flip side, if you're happy being naked in your dream it signifies a free spirit and confidence.

Searching for a toilet – being unable to find one, it's broken or is in public view – creates a heightened sense of urgency in a dream. It creates the same sense of exposure as it does in the naked dream, only this is even more embarrassing. We use the toilet for the natural elimination of body waste, and unless your body is telling you to get up and go the dream's message is usually to do with the need for release. Are you allowing yourself the basic necessities of life? Perhaps you crave more private space to take care of your needs or simply share your vulnerabilities with those you trust. Look at the situation in the dream: if the toilet is blocked or broken it may be time to examine the blockages in your life and what's no longer working.

If you dream about **falling** you may be experiencing a hypnagogic or hypnic jerk, which is a strong and sudden bodily contraction that occurs just as you're falling off to sleep. You may also have woken in fright from a dream with a stomach-churning feeling you were falling. If you're not experiencing a bout of vertigo it may be a physiological response: a drop in blood pressure or part of your body dangling out of the bed and not being supported. It is more common when you are in a chair rather than in your regular bed.

Symbolically, falling is associated with feeling unsupported, lacking in self-confidence and not being able to cope. Look at what's been going on in your life in previous weeks and examine areas where you're lacking support, then remove yourself from that situation or ask for help. Do you need to let go and take a leap of faith? Is the dream asking you to go with the flow despite being gripped by self-doubt and negative self-talk?

Drowning and rough waters such as big waves, tsunamis or flooding represent feelings of being overwhelmed emotionally. The feeling of powerlessness against such a force you have no control over usually reflects your waking life feelings. Are there ways to accept these feelings that involve surrender and lack of control? When you have no control over what happens to you in real life you have to relinquish it; if, for example, you have a terminal disease you can't control what happens to you but you can approach it with an attitude that is within your control.

Exams and tests are part of both waking and dreaming lives. We all have an innate need to achieve and compete for success, although in our working lives it can sometimes be difficult to accomplish. Your performance can have adverse effects on your employment, and your dreams will express this feeling of anxiety through scenes of exams and tests or a frustrating situation that reflects your real-life concerns.

If you dream of being unprepared for an exam, being late, going back to school, being in the wrong classroom or simply not understanding the exam paper, it may indicate a fear of failure and performance anxiety. Other versions of this dream theme include finding yourself in a situation in theatres or during a musical or sporting event in which you are unable to perform. You may feel you are being tested in real life and there is an expectation for you to perform well in a work situation or social event such as getting married, having children or owning a house.

The dream may be showing you that you are not prepared for the next step of your life, or it could simply be that you need to prioritise those things you need to work on harder. Think about whether you are avoiding learning a particular lesson in this lifetime. Are you repeating the same events, shown to you in your dream as school exams, and is it preventing you from advancing at a soul level for your growth?

Being late for an appointment is always stressful. When you see yourself frantically trying to either finish on time or get somewhere such as a funeral, wedding, sports event or the theatre on time it reflects your anxiety about failing to be there to take advantage of opportunities in life, whether it's professionally or in relationships. If you are in a space in your waking life where you are finding it difficult to make a decision and you knowingly are procrastinating, this dream is likely to appear.

Chase dreams are classic anxiety dreams representing primal fears that have existed since our prehistoric ancestors were being chased by animals or the members of other tribes. It's a familiar emotional response to the fight, flight or freeze situation we still experience emotionally. The chase dream theme represents feelings of insecurity: the figure that is chasing you is likely to represent those parts of yourself that are unresolved, repressed and neglected. If you are unable to move or are moving in slow motion while being chased it could mean you are in the natural paralysis of REM sleep.

If you dream of being chased, ask yourself what you are running away from and who is hounding you. If you face the pursuer – your real-life fears – in your dream instead of running away, you may gain insight into the cause of this distressing dream.

Teeth falling out is a metaphor for feeling vulnerable and not being in control. Carnivores have very powerful jaws and strong teeth, so we associate strength, power and control with healthy teeth. Teeth crumbling or falling out feels terrifying in your dream: you can't speak clearly, you can't eat and you look unattractive. You may be worried about your self-image or self-expression if your voice is not being heard or your feelings acknowledged. It might be that you are feeling intimidated by more assertive or aggressive people in your waking life.

All of the consequences of losing your teeth speak for themselves. Are you speaking your truth? Are you feeling vulnerable and not in control of a situation? Do you lack confidence in public? Have you been biting off more than you can chew? What major decision do you need to make but are hesitant to do so? There could be something you need to chew over.

If it's a recurring dream, note down when the theme appears: when you are experiencing the most self-doubt in unfamiliar situations such as in a new job, study or relationship, or when moving house or undergoing the responsibilities associated with being a carer or new parent.

Lost wallets or purses and valuables are emotionally charged anxiety dreams. Your purse or handbag not only holds your money, bank and credit cards but also your identification. When they are missing or stolen parts of yourself also go missing. How do you feel? What part of you have you lost? What are you searching for?

The dream is asking you to look at what you may potentially lose: your worth (money), your ID (purse), your home and car (keys) and relationships (pets, family) are just some symbols of the value you place on them. Sometimes dreaming of lost valuables creates a sense of loss, so they may appear during times of grief and loss in your real life.

Leaving baggage behind or your **luggage being lost** creates major stress and panic. Are you carrying emotional baggage that is best left behind? Maybe you need to lighten your load so you can move forward with greater ease and flexibility.

Missing body parts in a dream holds primitive fear as it means you're less equipped to survive. Hands are your tools for creation; your feet and legs take you where you need to go. Without these and other essential body parts you are missing parts of yourself. The Egyptian goddess Isis had the task of finding the dismembered body parts of her husband (or her own masculine side), Osiris, and it took much courage and effort to collect the parts to bring him to wholeness in order for him to live. What parts of yourself are you missing or cut off from you?

Death in dreams is not interpreted literally as a physical death. While dying in your dream may seem like the worst possible scenario, it is in fact a positive outcome as it generally means there is or will be an ending taking place, such as a job or relationship, moving out of your home or the end of old habits or belief systems, and that growth is occurring.

Look at whose death you are dreaming about. Dreams of the death of a parent, child, sibling or partner may represent change in the way you perceive or operate in those relationships. New self-discoveries are being made. The same applies to an ex-partner or school friends, with the dream simply reflecting the moving on from those times.

Dreaming of your own death suggests you are in transition and should reconnect with yourself and get ready for new changes coming your way, no matter how painful they seem at first. You are in transition.

ANIMALS

Animals represent your natural instincts, habits and personality, with each animal being unique to your relationship with that animal. In indigenous cultures animals are important totems and guides that carry messages and healing. Questions to consider when animals visit you in your dreams are who or what they represent in yourself and what do they want to teach you?

Domestic animals and pets keep us calm and make us feel less stressed. We have tamed animals that best suit our human needs for work and companionship, and usually associate domestic pets with specific characteristics: cats are independent, dogs are loyal and so on. Consider whether you need more of the qualities associated with particular animals and what parts of yourself have been tamed.

Each animal has a specific association that is universally common; the important thing to consider is their encounter with you in your dream. If you dream of a helpless, injured or young animal it could suggest a lack of self-care. Does this reflect your own emotional life? Are you nourishing yourself spiritually, mentally and physically?

Birds are universal symbols of freedom, expressed through the saying 'free as a bird'. They also represent an increased awareness and observations from a bird's eye view. Depending on the emotions experienced in the dream, you may be feeling caged in and longing for freedom. Ask yourself how you can best be free from obligations, expectations and a certain mind set, and how you can find your own voice.

Wild animals are untamed and free to roam in their primitive natural state. You may meet them in zoos, in your garden or in their natural habitats of jungle, savannah, forest, ocean, river, mountain or desert.

Wild animals are hardwired for survival, through a killer instinct or by camouflage and an ability to quickly flee. You may symbolically encounter the primitive killer instinct in you via an animal in your dream, having to fight for your life to survive in a way that you know is socially unacceptable but which lurks in the shadow of your subconscious. Dreaming of a wild animal is an opportunity to come face to face with parts of your wild, instinctual self you have kept hidden as well as identifying the characteristics of that animal's behaviour; for example, a lion's roar demonstrates the courage to show your anger.

Reptiles are ancient, prehistoric creatures that generally bring messages of healing to our dreams. Snakes are associated with trickery, deceit, sexual urges and danger and may be alerting you to potential threats in your waking life. A snake can kill or cure with its poison – the toxic compounds in snake venom have yielded new drugs that can treat anything from strokes to diabetes and cancer, for example – so as ancient messengers they represent healing, wisdom, the life and death cycle and transformation and renewal through shedding of the skin.

Humankind's relationship to snakes goes back to ancient times in worship and myths. A serpent was connected to the world tree of knowledge as the guardian of its secrets and mystical knowledge. The rod of Asclepius with the snakes entwined is a symbol of medicine and healing, and in kundalini yoga the snake is the energy centre coiled at the base of the spine. The Rainbow Serpent is part of the Dreamtime and creation story of Australian Indigenous tradition. It is a powerful force of nature: a life giver and protector of water and is associated with fertility.

Whether they are threatening or not in your dreams, snakes always bring wisdom. What do you need to learn from this ancient visitor?

A crocodile relies on its cunning and powerful jaws to snatch its prey; its attack is lethal both on land and in water. The fact that the prehistoric ancestors of the crocodile were the dinosaurs indicates this animal is incredibly adaptable to its environment. If you dream of a crocodile you are being asked to utilise cunning and be more adaptable in order to survive and thrive.

Insects are known for their traits of biting and stinging. Their bites and stings can be painful and toxic and compromise your health, so they represent things that bug you and drive you crazy. What small but painful annoyances do you have in your life? Do you feel danger from being swarmed or stung?

NATURE

Nature's elements are your internal weather station. Emotional storms, turmoil and unexpected eruptions symbolise big changes in your inner world. Collective human practices are bringing the living world to a dangerous level of extinction: forests are being logged so extensively it is causing the demise of ecosystems and animal species, oceans are being polluted with plastics and air is being polluted with chemicals and smoke. We seem to have lost balance in our natural world, which is reflected in what's going on in our own interior ecosystem.

If you dream of nature's elements, ask yourself what aspects you need to nurture and what elements nature teaches you about. What does your internal, emotional world look like? Do you treat nature respectfully or transactionally?

Dreaming about **storms, tsunamis and floods** is a good indicator of the level of turmoil you are experiencing in your waking life. Powerful changes are coming your way, but first the havoc and devastation wreaked by the storm suggest you are feeling powerless and out of control. Is your emotional life battering you? Are you close to drowning emotionally? You may need to wait for nature to restore calm and order before taking any steps to make changes.

Volcanic eruptions and exploding in anger are similar in intensity: tempers can flare and angry people's behaviour can pose a real risk to others. An outburst of unpredictable behaviour can be fierce and come without warning. Perhaps you know someone who has an explosive personality who is similar to a volcano: dormant most of the time but waiting to erupt? If you dream about volcanic eruptions you may need to let off steam and not suppress your anger lest it explodes and causes destruction.

Fire is both destructive and purifying when it turns the original material into ashes. It is a symbol of urgency, passion, transition and growth. What's urgent in your life that is causing you to feel under fire? Fire is transformative and thus it represents change: burning the old to welcome the new. Dreaming of fire is a means by which your psyche calls you to action and growth. If you've sustained a loss, a fire in your dreams suggests there is a new beginning coming.

Seasons reflect your mood or what phase of your life you are experiencing. Winter is a time of hibernation and incubation, and dreams of rain and snow indicate you are frozen or stalled when you want to move on with something. The dream is showing you that you are not ready yet to make progress. The seeds (new ideas, plans, goals, resolutions) are germinating but they won't be visible until spring.

Spring themes are often in images of bright colours, flowers, birds and generally a re-awakening time. You are experiencing a new phase or beginning. Summer is the height of activity and growth, so your psyche is experiencing a growth spurt and, with it, as sense of freedom and expression. Autumn is a time of harvest and abundance. With abundance comes a natural ending, as you notice colourful leaves on the ground. As they break down their nutrients penetrate the *soil*, ready to nourish the new seeds that will come up again in spring. If you take the seasons to be a metaphor of the stages of your life it will give you clues as to where you are at in the cycle.

❖ ACTIVITY PAGE ❖

Seasons, weather and the elements are symbols of
your internal life and moods. They represent the
cycles you are experiencing in terms of what phase
you are going through and how prepared you are.

JOURNALLING

Create a journal of four seasons to assist you with understanding
the transience of nature. You may wish to jot down all the words
you associate with each season, draw nature sketches of flora and
fauna, create poetry or cut and paste images that remind you of
that season. If you enjoy gardening, list all the vegetables, flowers,
insects, birds and wildlife of each season:

- Spring teaches you to be patient, to go slowly and gently just
  like when the first buds begin to open: if you force them to
  open too quickly they will bruise and wither. The mantra is
  'all in good time'.

- Summer teaches you to enjoy life to the fullest, to get
  together and have fun under the warmth of the sun.

- Autumn teaches you to rest. It is a season of transition, the
  in-between lull before the closing in of winter when you get
  a chance to catch your breath and contemplate your future.

- Winter teaches you that you are ready to let go of the old and
  wait for the new to begin.

Living in rhythm with the seasons resets your internal clock. Like the seasons your dreams have their own rhythms that prompt you to remain in sync and not rush through any stages of your life. The following haiku is an example of a simple yet imagery-rich observation:

Tree swaying
Branches lean and stretch
Into the grey atmosphere:
Autumn tango.

Write your observations in simple yet rich and evocative imagery.

VISUALISATION

Look at the detail in my bus journey visualisation below, which is representative of your dream state. The bus driver could be an emotion, a past-life experience or someone you are reminded of. Look beyond the exterior of everything you encounter in this visualisation, as these are your very own dream symbols.

I open my front entrance door and step outside my home, closing my door behind me. I walk through my garden and step onto the footpath beside my front gate. As I begin walking down this familiar street where I live, I see the sun's shining rays reflecting in the windows of the houses as I pass by.

After a short moment of walking I arrive at my bus stop at the end of my street. I sit down on a park bench seat and wait for my bus to arrive. While I wait I become aware of my surroundings where I sit. I feel a soft warm breeze gently swirl around me, and I hear birds happily singing in the trees behind me.

Then I see my bus has turned the corner of my street and is approaching me. I get up from the park bench seat and step to the curb. My bus stops in front of me and opens its doors for me to hop on. As I step onto my bus I look at the bus driver, and they smile at me. I pay my fare, then I walk down the aisle to choose a seat to sit down.

I notice my bus is filled with passengers. I see a vacant space three rows down and I sit there.

I look at the person I have sat next to, say hello and introduce myself. They greet me back and tell me their name, and we begin to chat and have a conversation. I take notice of what they look like, what clothes they wear, the colour of their hair and eyes and how their voice sounds. We talk while the bus travels around the city I live in.

After chatting for some time I see the beginning of my park at the end of my street approaching. I thank the person sitting next to me on the bus for our conversation. I stand up from my seat and press the next stop button, and walk to the front of the bus. As my bus comes to a halt at my bus stop I thank the bus driver. The doors open and I step off the bus.

I walk back up my familiar street to my house.

I walk through my garden up to my front door. I open my front entrance door and step inside my home, closing my door behind me.

RECONNECTING WITH NATURE

Ecological intimacy: there is a special intimacy when you kneel to plant seedlings in moist, fertile, black soil, take the first bite of a crisp, sweet apple off the tree, feel the velvety smooth moss enmeshed on a rocky surfaces or smell the scent of a rose in bloom. This earth relationship cannot be experienced online. Allow your senses to be flooded and discover the intimacy of being in nature.

Forest bathing: forest bathing is the practice of immersing yourself in nature in a mindful way, using your senses to derive a whole range of benefits for your physical, mental, emotional and social health. Take yourself for a walk in the park or, better still, a forest or bush where you can be alone and experience a close connection with nature touching trees, the earth and the grass and listen to the sounds of the bush. By reconnecting with nature you will be able to experience a meditative silence and reconnect to your own true nature.

PERSONAL RITUALS

Honour your dreams by bringing back an image and finding a place for it in your waking life. You may wish to paint a scene from your dream or write a poem out of the dream entry. Dreaming of wearing red shoes may trigger the memory of Dorothy in the movie *The Wizard of Oz.* You could watch the movie and repeat the mantra 'there's no place like home'.

If a deceased relative appears in your dream you might wish to light a candle for them. Place a photo of the deceased in front of the candle and make a note of their death anniversary or birthday.

Play a pretend game with your dream characters. If each character were your spirit guide, what would they teach you?

- ◎ the Uber driver (moves you round)

- ◎ the restaurant manager (is responsible for your nourishment)

- ◎ the council worker (takes care of your basic needs)

- ◎ the nurse (looks after your health)

- ◎ the bookkeeper (maintains balance in your life).

PERSONAL DREAM WORK

Emotions around people you meet in dreams: consider the idea that each time you dream of different people they teach you something both negative and positive about yourself or your life situation. Those people who have admirable qualities can inspire you, while those with destructive qualities motivate you to change.

To really notice people's messages in your dreams you need to focus on what they look like, say, do or make you feel, then when you bring that understanding back into the waking world you can try to figure out what the lesson is. Your goal is to try to learn as much as you can from this person or character.

The emotion you have when you wake up after a dream is a huge indicator of the dream's message. However, you will often focus on the action or the images to relay the bulk of the message. On the next page is a list of words to assist you in recalling the emotions you felt during the dream and upon waking. Circle any of the emotions you've experienced in your dreams that are related to the people you meet or know. These emotions are not limited to just one person but could be experienced in your dreaming of other people. Add any more to the list that apply to your dreaming.

After you circle the words re-imagine them into a creative source. For example, how would you like to feel in your waking life? If you have a sense of powerlessness, how would you change it into acceptance? You may use mantras, affirmations, artwork or dream re-entry as a creative means to acknowledge and then transform the experience into a positive one.

abandoned	accepted	accepting	adventurous	affectionate
aggressive	aimless	angry	annoyed	anxious
apprehensive	at ease	belonging	bitter	comforted
confident	conflict	conflicted	confused	connected
creative	critical	crushed	curious	defeated
determined	disappointed	discord	discouraged	disorganised
distress	distrustful	doomed	embarrassed	emptiness
excited	fearful of change	feeling like a failure	forgiving	free
frightened	frustrated	gloomy	guilty	harassed
heartbroken	helpless	hopeless	hostile	humiliated
hurt	impulsive	in danger	in survival mode	incompetent
independent	inferior	insecure	insignificant	instinctual
intimidated	intuitive	isolated	jealous	joyous
lonely	longing	loss	lost	loyal
melancholic	mistaken	mistreated	misunderstood	natural
needy	nostalgic	nourished	obsessive	optimistic
overlooked	overwhelmed	panic-stricken	persistent	pessimistic
playful	powerless	pressured	protective	reactive
regretful	rejected	resentment	run down	self-destructive
sense of loss	stressed	strong	struggling	stuck
suffering	surprised	threatened	tormented	trapped
uncertain	undeserving	uninhibited	uninspired	unstable
untamed	victimised	violated	vulnerable	weak
wistful	worried	worthless		

RECURRING DREAMS

It is frustrating to have dreams of recurring characters or situations and to have to deal with the emotional residue when you wake. Recurring dreams are usually associated with hidden or repressed trauma and are likely to show up when you move through significant phases of your life and are forced to deal with new situations that are out of your comfort zone.

Consider recurring dreams as signposts: look at the recurring theme and ask yourself how long you have been having the dream, when it began and when it usually comes up in a dream. Emotions are a good way to connect with the theme of a recurring dream, as you are able to more easily identify them.

DON'T
JUST
BE A
DREAMER,
BE A DREAM-
CATCHER!

Chapter 3

DREAMING DURING A WORLDWIDE PANDEMIC

'We're in a freefall into future ... And all you have to do to transform your hell into a paradise is to turn your fall into a voluntary act. It's a very interesting shift of perspective and that's all it is . . . joyfully participate in the sorrows of the world and everything changes.'

– JOSEPH CAMPBELL, *SUKHAVATI: A MYTHIC JOURNEY*, © JOSEPH CAMPBELL FOUNDATION

The world in 2020 experienced a cataclysmic event that will be recorded as an historical milestone for humanity. Our children's children will ask: 'How did you live in the time of COVID-19? Each day brought news of developments, with people watching their screens and checking their computers or phones with a sense of foreboding.

Not in our wildest dreams – or nightmares – could we have considered that countries would close their borders, air travel would be banned, schools shut and public gatherings outlawed. Hundreds of millions of people became unemployed and governments spent billions on stimulus packages. Working from home and home schooling became the norm, along with social distancing, lockdown, mandatory mask wearing and testing. Both the size and speed of what happened made our heads spin, and I'm sure we all questioned whether it was just a collective bad dream.

We could not have predicted that we as a modern civilisation would be gripped by an invisible enemy reminiscent of the voraciousness of the plagues we studied in our history lessons. The bubonic plague (or Black Death) killed around 50 million people, or 60 per cent of Europe's population, in the 14th century, while the 1918 influenza pandemic infected 500 million people and was responsible for an estimated 20 million deaths. At the time of writing COVID-19 had killed over a million people worldwide. This history of plagues was reflected in the trauma carried by so many in our collective memory.

During the COVID-19 pandemic city streets were empty, and there were no cacophonous sounds of trains, cars or planes. Around the globe was a stillness and silence never heard before, the pulsing of human activity simply a whisper. Mythologist Michael Meade describes it as a time when 'culture is collapsing at the same time that nature is unravelling – a rare time to be alive'.

> The common threat caused many people to readjust their values, to get back into balance as they understood the virus to be a catalyst for change. The pandemic brought us face to face with our mortality and that of others, and refocused our thinking to how we are intimately connected as a species, as a planet and as human consciousness.

HOW WERE WE AFFECTED IN WAKING LIFE AND THE DREAM WORLD?

The COVID-19 pandemic took its toll on everyone, resulting in high levels of stress, anxiety, suffering, depression and grief for millions around the globe.

Modern Western society often pushes hard-reality issues such as ageing, sickness and death into the background, but the pandemic forced us to collectively confront the harsh reality of our own and our loved ones' mortality.

> One significant and surprising indicator that the pandemic crisis affected us all was the increase and intensity of our dreams.

More people began posting on social media during lockdown to ask whether they were the only ones having bizarre and vivid dreams. Some claimed they were recalling dreams for the first time, and lack of sleep, disturbed sleep, nightmares, vivid dreams, exhaustion and anxiety were widely reported. Globally, people suffered from nightmares and anxiety dreams – or quarantine dreams, known as 'quarandreams'.

Dream researcher and psychologist Dr Deirdre Barrett from Harvard Medical School believes the global pandemic has created emotional and psychological problems for more than 30 per cent of the worldwide population, with symptoms such as post-traumatic stress disorder, nightmares, flashbacks, anxiety and difficulty sleeping. Studies have shown that events such as 9/11 and major natural disasters changed the way people dreamed for a period of time, making their dreams vivid and easy to recall in the following days and weeks. Dr Barrett reported that when people are directly involved in or witness a major traumatic event it strongly influences their dreams – the dream settings, scenes and storylines – during the time when the brain is resetting itself and processing the day's mental trash. This occurs predominantly during rapid eye movement (REM) sleep. Not surprisingly, the coronavirus pandemic had a similar impact on the dreaming mind at both an individual and collective level.

Studies suggest that our dreams are affected by our social environments during the day, which would explain why so many people dream about close friends and family in different situations that can be both positive and negative. Any dream that contains emotion is a dream the brain will file into its memory and give rise to recurring dreams about losing family and friends to the virus. Having to socially distance and isolate from social groups, colleagues, family and friends that would usually provide comfort and support and create memory circuits in the dreaming mind.

> The coronavirus caused us to experience a constant low-level stress. Even though technology such as Skype, Zoom, FaceTime or WhatsApp meant we weren't truly isolated while in quarantine, research shows that digital communication is no replacement for tactile, physical relationships. Human contact and connection are the very things humans need when in a state of suffering, and people's loneliness and sense of isolation increased during the pandemic and led to serious mental health issues.

How do these factors impact our dream world? Do we all dream collectively and share universal themes and dream images, or are there variations in dreams? Dreaming usually helps us cope with crises as our subconscious makes sense of them, but in a time of heightened alert our brains have much more to process during sleep and dreaming. The stress of lockdown, relationship and job security worries and a loss of all things familiar triggered emotional and terrifying dreams.

COLLECTIVE DREAMING

I am frequently asked, 'When am I dreaming my own dream and when is it a collective dream?'

The collective unconscious is part of our unconscious mind that holds ancestral memories, knowledge and experiences we share as a species, and is therefore the product of the repeated experiences of humanity. The collective unconscious means people worldwide dream similar dream images and themes that can also serve as a warning. Global dreams concerning disasters is a well-known phenomenon that has been observed and recorded by dream researchers, although it's not until after the events have occurred that the dreams have been verified.

I feel that as a race we have an innate intuition that is hardwired into our survival DNA. We are not conscious of it, but as someone who has lived in rural Australia and Europe I have observed the behaviour of wildlife before a storm, bushfire, flood or other natural disasters. Days before the smoke and fire from bush fires reach humans, birds in the Australian bush fly away to safety, some mammals shelter underground and others simply move on. I lived in an earthquake zone in Italy as a child and I remember the eerie silence of the birds and absence of animals before a major earthquake struck our town. Horses would pace restlessly and cows would upset milking buckets more readily. As humans we once utilised this collective intuition, the physical response to threats, to survive. Now we use technology to warn us of danger, so it is more of an unconscious collective experience.

Often people experience precognisant dreams that foretell a future event or describe the details exactly. Collectively, dreamers had similar dreams prior to the 2020 Venice floods, as they did with other natural disasters such as the major earthquakes and tsunami in 2011 in Japan.

The threat of the virus insidiously entering into our subconscious led to more anxiety dreams where the dreamer experienced fear, embarrassment, social taboos, work-related stress, grief and loss, as well as terrifying literal dreams centring on contamination, disease and death. The increase in anxiety dreaming was to be expected: similar experiences have been reported during times of sudden changes, uprisings, anxiety and trauma, such as in the aftermath of terrorist attacks, natural disasters and war. Whether these traumatic events were experienced first hand or through reporting via the media, it resulted in the generation of escalating vivid dreams.

WHY DID WE REMEMBER DREAMS MORE?

What was odd about some of the pandemic dreams wasn't only their content or the fact that they were more vivid but that we remembered them, which isn't typical. We normally forget most of our dreams shortly after waking up unless we write them down.

The increase in vivid dreams could be explained by the changes the pandemic forced on people's lifestyles. Disruption in your routine may disturb your circadian rhythm (the 24-hour cycles that are part of the body's internal clock), which would then disrupt your sleep. Keeping constantly updated on the news from waking up until falling asleep can also contribute to restless nights and the frequency of dreams.

Alcohol disrupts your sleep cycle and can interfere with your REM sleep. For many, drinking alcohol typically suppresses the memories of dreams, but drinking more often can have the opposite effect of waking us up during REM sleep, which is the deep phase of sleep when our brains are most active. This will in turn make our dreams more vivid and more easily remembered.

To explain in more detail: during the first part of the night alcohol increases non-REM sleep (including deep sleep) and suppresses

REM sleep, but as the blood alcohol level drops in the second half of the night the reverse happens: sleep is shallower and waking becomes more frequent. This results in higher dream recall and more REM sleep, which leads to vivid dreams and nightmares.

REM AND DISRUPTED SLEEP

When we sleep we go through different stages that cycle throughout the night, waking up briefly at the end of each 90-minute sleep cycle. This includes light and deep sleep and a period known as rapid eye movement (REM) sleep, which we experience more in the second half of the night. Dreams can occur within all sleep stages.

We generally have several REM dream periods during a night although we do not necessarily remember them. The most intense period of REM sleep usually takes place just before waking up in the morning, so if you're sleeping in later because you're out of work or working from home it's more likely you'll experience longer, deeper periods of REM and have more vivid dreams.

REM sleep has unique properties that help to regulate mood, performance and cognitive functioning.

During REM sleep the areas of the brain responsible for emotions, memory, behaviour and vision are reactivated, as it's in the REM sleep stage that we have the most vivid dreams.

I have heard people say 'I am getting my sleep but I'm so tired', while others state they dream in fragments instead of complete sequences. These statements echo my own experiences and it feels to me that day-time anxieties spill over into my sleep and dream time.

If anxiety is negatively impacting your sleep your brain may try to catch up on REM sleep (called rebound sleep) whenever it can, creating more spurts of vivid dreaming throughout the night. This was why so many people experienced vivid and mostly emotionally disturbing dreams during the pandemic. Naturally, when we experience fear and anxiety in our waking lives the emotions will slip into our night dreams. Dr Barrett says that during the pandemic there was a cluster of dreams that revolved around getting the virus, exposing feelings of fear, loss, destruction, lack of control, falling apart, isolation and grief.

Dream experts agree such widespread collective dreaming and our ability to share it in real time were unique in human history – both in waking time and in dreaming time. And you, the dreamer, are part of these combined realities.

COMMON DREAM THEMES DURING THE PANDEMIC

In the following section are examples of the most common dream themes and their variations during the global pandemic.

CATCHING OR DYING FROM THE VIRUS

The most obvious dream was one that carried on from that day's anxiety: catching the virus. People had dreams in which they were spiking a fever, catching the virus, and/or dying from it, with respiratory distress causing an inability to breathe.

Research undertaken by US-based dream analyst Lauri Loewenberg suggests the stress of lockdown, relationship concerns and a loss of all things familiar triggered emotional and surreal night-time encounters ranging from dreams of bugs and natural disasters to some experiencing physical pain. Many reported dreams of survival that reinforced the rule of social distancing. Ominous scenes included the dreamer screaming to 'keep away', running away from people trying to cough on them or from dangerous situations or being unable to breathe due to lungs filling with fluid, all of which reflected the fear of not surviving the pandemic. Although the function of dreams is to keep us safe, we forget this while experiencing survival nightmares. In our nightmares the danger of dying feels very real.

Less common were positive dreams where if someone got the virus they would go and find a miracle potion that cured it. Positive outcomes of dreams are particularly relevant to the younger demographic due to their sense of invincibility, although are not necessarily experienced by this age group. During the time of the coronavirus a significant number of younger people disregarded the distancing laws and continued their social lives, attending parties and going to the beach and nightclubs – playing the game of cheating or denying death and thinking the virus would only affect older people.

The most common dream was one with elderly parents and grandparents dying, and not surprisingly as the virus was most deadly among the older population. Some people feared their family or friends would catch the virus, survivor's guilt being a dream's way of expressing real-life frustration about being separated from loved ones. Others dreamed of being unable to breathe, again a realistic dream based on the medical fact that difficulty breathing was the most frightening symptom of the virus.

Another common dream thread was a threat to work or financial status, including dream scenarios of not finding their workplace, being locked out of homes, leaving the trolley at the supermarket filled with groceries or, conversely, being unable to reach the trolley due to obstacles such as crowds. This was a reflection of the financial crisis the world experienced during the pandemic.

In general, dreams are very sensitive to collective feelings that the world is turning chaotic or ending, which is why many people experienced end-of-time dreams.

APOCALYPTIC DREAMS

I requested 'dreams experienced during COVID-19' on social media, and it was fascinating to delve into the mind's imagination during this torrid time in our history.

> I'm often dreaming of hand sanitiser and yelling at people for not being socially distant. I also keep dreaming that the virus is almost zombie like, that if it touches you you're dead within seconds and all bloody and gross!

It's clear that our anxieties about the virus crept into our dreams. A zombie apocalypse was the perfect thing for the subconscious mind to manifest at such a stressful time. The longer the restrictions continued the scarier it became in the conscious mind, and when the dreaming mind tries to process these feelings it inevitably leans on horror movies that are visually terrifying. Zombies are a metaphor for people partially living their lives: they are there but not really communicating, which sounds very much like how it was during the time of COVID-19.

DROWNING OR NATURAL DISASTERS

Drowning and natural disasters formed another collective dream theme during the pandemic. The earth symbolises our own nature, where we felt overwhelmed and unable to contain our feelings. Water-based disasters are more common, as water in this context represents sadness and worry. One dreamer who responded to my dream request said:

> I was drowning in an underground car park filling with water.

CHILDREN MISSING, HURT OR IN DANGER

Children missing, being abducted, hurt or in danger was another top pandemic theme that relates to the real-life fear of losing a family member to the virus or missing out on aspects of a child's or grandchild's normal lives. Dreams can dredge up feelings about being threatened or not being able to protect kids who are out of control or in accidents:

> Last night I dreamed that my youngest child rode past me on a low drift trike with a surfboard under his arm. Then he went off down a hill that had a sharp turn at the bottom and his trike sped up and he didn't make the turn and slammed into a pub, and then he was lying in the road and everyone was trying to help him but I couldn't run down the hill to help him. I just stood there, calling his name.

Watching a crash is more painful for the parent than for the child as you can't hurry the healing process once they get hurt and you can't fix things for them. More than ever during a world crisis parent protective emotions kick in at high gear, with the overall message seeming to be: let go of things you can't control.

DEATH

Death – not surprisingly – is by far the most common universal pandemic dream. Social distancing is contrary to human nature, but millions of people were cut off from family and friends except through social media and other technological, distant connections. Tragically, many mortally ill people passed away without ever having direct contact with or seeing their loved ones, but the most vivid and disturbed dreams came to those on the front line who witnessed first hand the distress, desperation and death caused by the outbreak.

There were visitation dreams from those who had passed on, some of them pleasant and others a little strange. We faced our own mortality and prepared for our inevitable death, which our dreams facilitated via our loved ones who had passed on greeting us from the other side. Visitations from ancestors, mythic figures, superheroes or angelic or spiritual beings appear to us in dreams to offer comfort.

More people dreamed of survival, in dreams that reinforced safe social distancing. The function of dreams is to keep us safe, and the following two dreams are an interesting example of how death was expressed through dreams during the pandemic:

> I was in a café when my mother, who has passed away, came to sit down next to me. She carried a mask made from our old curtains. She laid it on the table and said, 'Oh, I don't need to wear it. I'm dead.'

> It was a really clear dream. There were four hearses with trailers on the back, with a white mesh covering on the trailer. There were more hearses ahead in the distance. It was an open road, and I was told by someone in the car I was driving to

pull over. I said I was going to flat country open road, so that
didn't apply to me. I was aware that there was one body in
the hearse ahead of me and one in the trailer. Some military
men were in charge. My overall feeling in the dream was that
I was being controlled.

The hearses are symbols of death, but an interesting feature is the white mesh covering the trailers. The dreamer said the mesh reminded her of hospital masks, so we can assume her subconscious mind was pointing to the fact that people in the hearse and trailers had died due to the coronavirus. With regard to the open spaces and the military, in order for lockdown laws to be enforced police and military personnel were often stationed at major highway points and at border closures to protect those living in the rural countryside. The dreamer lived in the country and therefore the open spaces represented her freedom and getting away from the controlled atmosphere of the city and the military.

METAPHORS IN DREAMS

Apart from the obvious connection between waking life and pandemic-related dreams, universal dream themes used metaphors for conveying messages to the dreamer. Dream themes that increased in intensity included running away from wild animals, rats, bug or snake bites, aliens, being chased and falling.

The usual meaning of these typical anxiety dreams still applied, but it was significantly relevant to the dreamer's personal experiences. Wild animals suggest fear and vulnerability for the dreamer; seeing rats is about lack of trust and resourcefulness; aliens (or being lost somewhere) reflect the difficulties of having to deal with something totally foreign; bug or snake bites is our primitive brain kicking in to remind us of exactly how toxic and potentially lethal the virus was; and falling indicated a general feeling of helplessness.

WILD ANIMALS OR MONSTERS

Wild animals or monsters are the dreaming mind's way of making sense of the concept of 'uncontrollable forces' experienced in waking life. Sensing the presence of a monster but not being able to see it is reminiscent of the days when as children we would fear the monster under the bed or see spooky shadows on the wall made by the wind blowing in the tree branches outside the window, or the terrifying dressing gown cord dangling out of the wardrobe door with its snake-like form.

When it is dark in a dream it's often because the dreamer's emotions are uncertain or they are in the dark about certain issues that are occurring. The dreamer's subconscious uses effective memory images that are emotionally charged to get their conscious attention and give form to the virus.

> I have a recurring dream where it's dark and there's a monster in the room, and I can't really see it. I can feel it and hear its heavy breathing. I can sense it getting closer, and right before it attacks me I wake up.

The invisible force (in this case the coronavirus) that is a monster and is capable of killing without the victim being prepared is reality in disguise.

> I dream I am facing a bull. It's coming to attack me and there's nowhere for me to go.

A charging bull is a formidable symbol of strength and perseverance, as can be observed in the running of the bulls in Spain and in bull-fighting rings and rodeos. The qualities the virus closely resembles are its aggressive and unshakeable grip on the victim, who is unprepared to deal with the mighty force of a (symbolic) charging bull.

BUGS AND INSECTS

A cluster of bugs of the same type are the most common: flying insects such as locusts, wasps, bees, mosquitoes and other group of insects such as cockroaches and spiders, all attacking or running at the dreamer.

In dreams bugs can easily be understood by the human language nickname for infectious germs and viruses being referred to as 'bugs' or from the saying 'catching a bug'.

I was woken up at 4.46 am in a dream where a big ant was trying to bite me; the dream was so real. My husband was also woken by a swarm of bees chasing him and trying to sting him and my teenage daughter reported that at 5 am she dreamed she was being chased by a massive spider trying to bite her.

SNAKES

Like bugs, snakes 'bite' and often their bite can be deadly. Likening it to a venomous reptile simply reflects the fear of catching the virus.

I was repeatedly bitten by a snake while I was in a large fish tank.

I was attacked by a snake launching itself at me.

WAR, VIOLENCE AND LAW BREAKING

Dreaming of violence involving shooting or explosions is a message from the dream state that the dreamer is in danger.

> I had a weird dream where I was dangerous and wanted by the police, but I wanted to get a book from the library and the librarian recognised me and panicked and ran screaming from the library. There were some other messy bits with people afraid of me and running away too.

In a normal dream interpretation the dreamer may want to reflect on the police and librarian as figures of authority and what they represent. Does the dreamer respect them? I would ask: if the people in this dream represent parts of you, what would they actually represent? Do you need to police something more carefully? Are you organised in your work habits?

During pandemic dreaming the police and librarian represent the law and what constitutes law breaking: not social distancing, refusing to wear a mask, going out while waiting for COVID test results. Fear of not adhering to laws and the consequences of doing so are played out in this dream. People running away screaming suggests the dreamer may be suspected of having the virus.

THEME PARKS, SPORTS STADIUMS AND LARGE PUBLIC PLACES

Theme parks, sports and entertainment stadiums and large public spaces were empty during the pandemic. The loss of fun and social interactions gained from attending concerts, sports and theme parks is a strong emotion the conscious mind retains and files into the subconscious dreaming mind. This adds to collective feelings of loneliness and isolation and an understanding of the seriousness of the pandemic.

I am at Disneyland. It's empty. I run around trying to get on the rides, but nothing is functioning. It's eerie.

Disneyland and anything connected with Disney is a symbol of childhood innocence, fun, laughter and the good old days. When nothing is functioning it suggests that things have changed; in other words, what used to work no longer does and is now not safe. The subconscious mind is coming to terms with a different situation from the norm and finds it challenging to make the pandemic lifestyle work.

I am trapped in an outdated theme park where nothing works like it should. The only way out is to queue with others and go on a type of slide upwards to the top and hopefully not find the upstairs fenced off or blocked.

Being trapped in queues or upside down and a topsy-turvy slide are images that represent waking life challenges, emotions of being trapped inside the home and everything not being normal and functioning the way it should or did. Nothing makes sense, and the queues indicate a sense of being controlled.

INTRUDERS AND INVISIBLE OR UNCONTROLLABLE ENTITIES

COVID-19 spread quietly and invaded unsuspecting hosts, similar to what an intruder or invisible entity or monster does. Its insidious nature created the intruder or invisible entity attack dream image and scenarios of invasion, intrusion, lack of control and invisibility.

I have had a recurring dream where an intruder attacks me, knife pressed against my neck, and I am holding my breath ready to die. This came back during the pandemic. I can't see the intruder, only darkness and the inevitability of death.

I was at my art class, sketching a hand which then came to life on the easel. I had no control over it. The hand sketched my son in the bath tub: it was reaching forward to grab my young son as he fell into the hot water tub. I raced home on a weird rail network that required me to push along on my hands and knees, frantic the whole time. When I raced upstairs my son was lifeless on the bottom of the bath. I reached down and dragged him out in one swoop, sat him on the floor and pushed on his chest and water bubbled out of his mouth. At that point I woke up, so distraught, literally crying, and the feeling would just not leave me.

Anxiety for children's safety was dialled to high as parents navigated the constant juggle of regulations and changes with child care and schools during the pandemic. Emotions either came bubbling to the surface and needed to be discussed or were pushed down. Dreads and fears that are suppressed and not acknowledged eventually cause the psyche to feel disconnected.

The hand that came to life is an unseen force that can be used for good or for destruction; it may represent the dreamer's own anxiety about whether or not they are doing enough to take care of their child. Imagine a hand-sketched hand that could take care of the family: that would be a hero's secret weapon or special power.

The strange rail network on which the dreamer was frantically moving on hands and knees to reach the child in danger indicates common obstacles facing scientists, whose search for a vaccine moved at a frantic pace.

OLD DREAMS RESURFACING

Dreams can be triggered by old trauma as well as life during the pandemic. When the old trauma and the new stressful situation coincide, dreams become intensified and terrifying.

> *I've had a dream I used to have when I was a kid. It used to happen at 11 pm or 12 midnight each night: I was held under a wave of water, unable to breathe and unable to get to the surface. The water was much denser than normal and it was like this was happening to me at a cellular level where I became a part of the effervescent turbulent water.*

Emotions resurface from childhood nightmares and old traumas are replayed. Water indicates big emotional changes, so feeling trapped under water means the dreamer is feeling overwhelmed, disempowered, emotionally shut down or being made to feel they can't express themselves, which in turn makes the dreamer feel out of control. When you are unable to breathe in a dream, whether it's water or suffocation of any sort, it suggests your lifeline and individuality are being compromised.

When any dream resurfaces you are facing the same emotional challenges and feelings now you felt in the original dream. The turbulence of life mirrors the turbulent wave. In the second part of the dream where the water was denser and the dreamer became part of the effervescent turbulent water is an encouraging sign from the psyche that the dreamer is or will become part of the solution. Through the turbulence the dreamer will overcome the struggle and become part at a cellular level of the effervescent water.

We were not in control of our lives during the stressful period of the pandemic and it's natural that old dreams would resurface, but you must look at them with a fresh perspective, revisit them and heed their messages.

BEING LOST AND ESCAPE DREAMS

Being in a place you don't recognise and feeling lost or trying to find people, and parents dreaming of looking for their children and needing to be with them are all dreams that represent feeling disoriented. We had to live in a world we didn't recognise and looked for normality to make a comeback.

A sense of being lost or finding things you've never known or experienced before is part of experiencing a completely different set of circumstances that had to be adapted to on a daily basis. Dreaming of being in a familiar city but not recognising it is another way your subconscious mind processes change.

> *I had a full movie dream last night: a family of six had to get out of the city because there was some threat, and the eldest child, the mum and the baby died. The dad was elsewhere and the middle two kids tagged along with a rough old woman to escape, except something happened once they got out and time reversed and they were all back in the city again alive and well. Only the middle girl knew they had to escape immediately or three of them would die, but everyone else was like: oh, wait and see! But even the middle girl was beginning to doubt that anything was terribly wrong and was looking for the rough old woman to confirm that things had really happened and they did have to escape.*

Getting out and escaping the city in the time of COVID-19 (the threat) is a dream of self-preservation where there are likely to be fewer people and less chance of being infected. Interestingly, the eldest child, mother and baby died and the father was absent, which could indicate the dreamer's psyche had to use alternative ways to survive than those on offer.

As a generalisation middle children are known for their difficult personalities or inventiveness, and it's possible these qualities were the ones needed. It's also possible that taking the middle ground or using common sense regarding information on COVID-19 was necessary. The dreamer doubts herself as there is a barrage of information and not all of it is accurate. The dreamer's inner wisdom knows what's right but she has lost confidence. The dream's message comes from deep wisdom: don't doubt your common sense and remain centred.

During the pandemic people felt their most vulnerable and were afraid of not being in control of their lives or their decisions. There was a palpable fear at a collective level of social uprisings along with a lack of trust in people who held positions of power and influence, mixed with conspiracy theories and fake news. It pushed everyone out of their comfort zone and was a tinderbox waiting to be lit.

RIOTS AND DISASTERS

In days and weeks after the death of George Floyd in the United States and the resulting Black Lives Matter protests against racial injustice, a survey was conducted on recurrent themes in people's dreams about the ongoing rioting and world protests. The common theme about protestors, police, acts of violence and destruction reflected the reality of the news reports. There was a difference now in the focus of dreamers' anxiety and distress.

Some were haunted by police aggression and images of George Floyd's horrific death. For others it was the threatening nature of attacks on family homes or businesses by the rioters and looters.

The worst dream scenes involved the protests merging with the pandemic; it consisted of being part of the protest but terrified of being too close to other people.

In Australia the destructive December/January bushfires had just abated when we heard the news of COVID-19 infiltrating the world. Confused and apprehensive, we awoke from the daze of one nightmare only to be confronted by something even more catastrophic. It made us recalibrate our lives, our values and our perspectives. If we were careful not to consume too much media information and didn't become overwhelmed by our fears we could find ways to survive and sometimes even thrive.

Every dream has multiple meanings, some of which take time and reflection to recognise and digest. Both literal and symbolic meanings are valid when working out a dream.

> Dreams don't solve our problems, but they do give us a glimpse of what those problems are and ways in which we can create changes.

In times of global crises, dreams offer a valuable insight into the collective condition and raise awareness of our interconnectedness.

Horrific events and experiences in real life translate as a form of post-traumatic stress disorder (PTSD) in dreams. Dr Barrett, who has researched and written scientific papers about stress over disasters being manifested in dreams, believes the mind can re-route itself during sleep and dreaming times so that dreams de-fuse any stressful events experienced in waking life.

When we experience a difficult situation that affects so many both our conscious and unconscious bodies also pick it up. Collective traumatic situations trigger old personal traumas, and combined can create a perfect storm that may then result in nightmares, anxiety and potential mental health issues.

SILVER LININGS: A BRIGHTER FUTURE

It's a virus, yes . . . in the midst of this terrible despair, it offers us a chance to rethink the doomsday machine we have built for ourselves. Nothing could be worse than a return to normality. Historically, pandemics have forced humans to break with the past and imagine their world anew. This one is no different.

– ARUNDHATI ROY

Many people agree that returning to the life we had before COVID-19 would be detrimental to our evolution. What we had is no longer globally sustainable, and when a disaster rips open the fabric of normality we glimpse possibilities of another world that is aligned with humanity's best traits. We now have a chance to unite with one another and reconnect with the deep wisdom of the earth.

Grandmother Bernadette Rebienot from the International Council of Thirteen Indigenous Grandmothers reminds us of the importance of life: 'Human beings are endowed with intelligence but, despite their desire to dominate nature, the latter will always triumph. Let us remember that the central element is Life. It's up to us to keep the flame alive.'

The very best of humanity and a taste of nature unrestrained by human chains can be experienced through a greater sense of human connection, solidarity and compassion, clear skies, an opportunity for reflection and introspection, loud bird song and deer roaming a country lane. The pandemic shone a light on our need for interconnectedness and interdependency as we adjusted to a vastly different world. Dreams have the capacity to bring healing to our bodies and our psyche, although we must first heal ourselves of old wounds that appear in our dreams in terrifying shapes and images.

Amor fati is a Latin phrase meaning the 'love and embrace of one's fate' or, in simpler terms, a love of what happens. Unlike destiny, in which we pursue a quest for fulfilment, *amor fati* treats each and every moment as something to be embraced rather than avoided. When we accept that things happen outside our control we will learn to be okay with it. Actually, more than okay – we should have *amor fati*.

❖ ACTIVITY PAGE ❖

TIPS FOR BETTER DREAMS

During any time of restricted social activity when your physical body may be confined to your home your dream body and mind are still free to wander in whatever places they wish to go. You can practise this through waking visualisations, meditations, daydreams and night-time dreaming.

◎ Be inventive and imagine what you would rather dream about. As you're drifting off to sleep, tell yourself what imagery you want to dream about and begin to imagine what it would look, feel, sound, taste and smell like. Are you at the beach, the forest, a lake or mountain? Who are you with? This imagery will seep into your dreaming mind. It's called dream incubation, where you set the intention to dream whatever you wish.

◎ Remove excess fear and notice beauty around you, because when you are over-fearful you create more fear in the world. Everyone vibrates differently when they are in fear mode, and one way to release fear is to calm your senses. Do whatever works for you: walking where and when you can, being in nature, bringing nature to you with lots of plants, watching a nature program or burning candles or oils that are plant based. Listen to a favourite uplifting book as an audio or music.

◎ Create a possible future. Just as you can incubate dreams and influence what you dream about, the same applies to dream scenarios. (A dream scenario is a dream that has a full scene, usually with a loose beginning, middle and end. Most of the time dreams come in fragments without beginnings or endings.) You can do this in your normal waking state, ideally when you are relaxed and have time set aside to do it.

◎ Create desirable future scenarios out of your anxiety or dream state. Your subconscious is open to suggestive prompts: the more you feed it suggestions the more it will take them seriously and store them for a time when it's possible to realise or manifest these future scenarios. What does your dream home, partner or job look like? Where do you want to travel to that you haven't already visited? Focus on a past holiday you enjoyed.

◎ There are ways to change dream endings if you are willing to persevere with the practice of conscious dreaming. You don't need to go to sleep in order to dream; your most powerful dreaming may unfold in the twilight zone between asleep and awake.

◎ Keep a dream journal, which is essential if you are at all interested in dreams. We forget most of our dreams on waking even though we think at the time we will remember them. Date each entry and give it a title, as this is going to become the most important book on dreams you will ever read. It is going to be an oracle book of your personal symbols that will enable you to create a data log of your dream history. It is an intimate sharing of lessons from your inner self.

DREAM
BIG.

Chapter 4

LIVING YOUR STORY THROUGH SYNCHRONICITY AND DREAMS

'We have, each of us, a life story, an inner narrative — whose continuity, whose sense, is our lives. It might be said that each of us constructs and lives a "narrative," and that this narrative is us, our identities.'

— OLIVER SACKS, *THE MAN WHO MISTOOK HIS WIFE FOR A HAT*

Dreams are not just flights of imagination; they are an essential part of our lives that bring us hope and purpose and enable us to create a bigger vision of who we want to be. They allow us to have a sense of purpose and meaning about who we are and what we do. If you never remembered a single dream, how would you know what was possible? How would you be inspired and what would fuel your dreams? Your waking life dreams and your night dreams work together to encourage your passions and creativity and help you make better life choices.

SYNCHRONICITY

Synchronicity, or meaningful coincidences, is a phenomenon we have all experienced where spirit and matter connect. You dream of a fox and the next day you unexpectedly see one. You are made redundant and out of the blue a former employer calls to offer you a new job. You get off at the wrong train station and meet up with your long-lost love. As unlikely as it may sound, spirit and matter are connected.

In *waking dreams* such as these the time construct collapses; your calendar and internal clocks no longer apply. Many indigenous cultures view time as being a more circular pattern: one that can bend to the individual, who is at the centre of that synchronistic experience. When you are lucky enough to experience synchronicity your life no longer seems to be a random set of events but rather a life with value and purpose. You glimpse the acorn that exists within along with the potential to become the mighty oak.

'Nothing happens in which you are not entangled in a secret manner, for everything has ordered itself around you and plays your innermost. Nothing in you is hidden to things . . .

The stars whisper your deepest mysteries to you, and the soft valleys of the earth rescue you in a motherly womb.'

– CARL JUNG, *THE RED BOOK*

It was analytical psychologist Carl Jung who introduced the concept of 'synchronicity'. He was aware at all times of the signs and symbols around him, whether it was the flight pattern of birds, the wind direction on water over a lake or the unexpected appearance of a wild animal in his path. All of these factors gave him insight into the universal symbols a person's psyche dreams up. Synchronicities, dreams, daydreams, serendipity and coincidences are not random; they are insights, information, knowledge, wisdom and truths presented to you as signs and exist to demonstrate there is more to you than you are aware of.

Everything happens for a reason and, even if you are uncertain of the reasoning behind it, there is a deep truth to it.

When you as a dreamer are given glimpses of synchronicities they present as puzzle pieces, a trail of breadcrumbs that encourage you to delve, to seek, to know.

They are reminding, awakening and enlivening you to consciously be aware that you are connected to and part of something much greater than simply your mortal self, that you are more than the total sum of where you were born, how much money you have, your job and any other classification you have been given or that you impose on yourself and others. The higher powers wish to gain your attention and give you pieces along your life journey so you can acknowledge and understand the bigger picture.

To repeatedly encounter synchronicities is to be in alignment, to be consciously aware and awake in life similar to living a dream or experiencing a dream-like reality. You may downplay the value of these encounters because they aren't understood by your logical mind, but they exist to connect with you at an intuitive level. The ancients lived their truth: with mists swirling around them they entered an altered state in which they became one with nature, trees, the environment and the cycles of the seasons.

I once had a calling to visit Glastonbury to follow my quest. For my journey I asked a priestess or guardian energy to accompany me and along the way show me signs as a confirmation of the purpose of my visit. As I drove through the majestic landscapes on the way to the Cornwall coastal sacred site of Saint Michael's Mount I visually held on to the image Excalibur, the sword of truth, to remind myself of my authenticity as a seeker. Signs began to appear in succession beginning with Rose Cottage, a lovely bed and breakfast with a beautiful rose garden in all colours; then past Rose Avenue and on to a hamlet called Rose, and finally a sign leading to Roseland Peninsula. By now I was convinced of the power of signs and synchronicities that reaffirmed my purpose by showing me my name at every instance. It is only because I gave it my attention that I became an observer and allowed synchronicity to guide me.

LIMINAL SPACES

Dreams invite multiple access points or doorways through which you can enter the dream state. Liminal spaces through which you can enter the dream state are via hypnagogia and hypnopompia.

Hypnagogia is the transitional state of wakefulness before falling asleep, a consciousness state known generally as the twilight zone. You will be familiar with this state because it's the space between waking and dreaming when your mind has not quite shut down but your body is totally relaxed. Some people have reported seeing psychedelic images or hearing strange auditory sounds and voices in this in-between state of consciousness.

It's common to have an encounter with the deceased in dreams in the liminal space of hypnagogia. The dead appear as they are: not in ghostly forms but how you remembered them, and they often look much younger and healthier than they were when they passed on. These visitation dreams can be comforting as you feel reassured that 'life' continues in another dimension.

Hypnopompia is opposite to hynagogia as it is the consciousness state you are in immediately before you wake up, taking place between dreaming and waking. It is a state of consciousness in which your extrasensory perception is strong and important messages are channelled through you. People report this is also a time they are likely to come into contact with the spirit world and receive great insights.

The science of dreams teaches us that dreams are responses to our daily lives in which our brains process the excess material we can't deal with in our waking lives. Your dreams have greater plans for you than to simply take out your mental trash and replay your anxieties. Even when your ordinary life is uneventful your dream scenarios will play out like a movie in which you are creating a bigger story of your life.

Psychologist and writer James Hillman says we are born with a code written into our soul. He compares it to an acorn, which contains the entirety of the oak tree programmed within it: each of us has a fate written into us from birth into which we will grow. This code is our individual guiding force or spirit called a 'daemon', one that looks after us and guides us to keep us safe in life and on track to fulfil our destiny. Are the images structured in our dreams clues to the fate that has already been programmed?

It's therefore essential to pay attention to your dreams, as each acorn is a potential oak tree and each tree creates a forest: every individual dream is a piece of a jigsaw puzzle that will dream a better world into wholeness. You don't dream just for yourself but for the collective tribe: all of humanity. Your guiding force joins another's guiding force so we all end up with the same force.

When do you know you are connected to a dream world in which your daemon is present? Think of those times when you woke up from a big dream in tears or were frightened or elated and it made you feel sick, lonely, depressed and unhappy with your life. As it is your physical body that sleeps and not your emotional body, which is switched on 24/7 and always experiencing emotions, you can feel real emotions when you wake from your dreams. The emotions you feel when you are awake transfer into your dreams, giving you information to act upon.

ASCLEPIUS' SLEEP TEMPLES

Our ancestors recognised that we can see the future in dreams. How many times have you recognised the connection between your night's dreams and your general dreams and hopes? The ancients understood three essential elements about dreams:

- Dreams give you a direct link to the sacred, to gods and goddesses, ancestors and animal totems.

- Dreams offer you the opportunity to heal yourself, showing you which parts of your body are in need of attention.

- Dreams show you the state of your soul and whether you need to retrieve those vital parts of yourself that may have gone missing. Shamans call this 'soul loss' and use the practice of soul retrieval to bring it back.

Most ancient cultures had a deep understanding of the dream world as being a real world, even more real that the waking world. The ancient Egyptians believed that in dreams our eyes are opened and therefore we are 'awake'.

Dreams were so significant to the lives of people in many ancient cultures that they built elaborate temples for dream incubation dedicated to their healer: Imhotep in Egypt and Asclepius in Greece. These gods were recognised as having the power to cure people of a variety of ailments within sleep and their sacred dreams. People travelled long distances to go to the temples and would adhere to the strict preparation rules from the priests – fasting, purification rituals, sacrificial offerings and drinking only from pure mineral springs – before lying down in a sacred dream chamber.

In ancient Greece sleep temples gave people a direct link to the gods and goddesses in order to heal mind, body and spirit; the idea of being in harmony in mind, body and spirit was vital to the ancient Greek notion of health.

The most famous sleep temple was the original temple of Asclepius, the son of Apollo, the Greek god of music. Asclepius' mother was the mortal princess Coronis, who was tragically slain by Apollo in a jealous rage for her infidelity with the mortal Ischys. Asclepius was cut from his dead mother's womb as she lay on a burning funeral pyre. Asclepius was raised and taught the arts of medicine by the centaur Chiron. Being a demi-god, Asclepius was gifted with divine healing powers and was able to communicate with snakes. Zeus, the father of the gods, was angered when Asclepius abused his powers to bring dead men back to life and punished Asclepius with a deadly thunderbolt strike. After Asclepius' death Zeus placed his body among the stars as the constellation Ophiuchus. He was later reinstated as a god on Olympus and became known as the serpent-bearing dream healer god. The rod of Asclepius, a snake-entwined staff, remains a symbol of medicine today as the caduceus.

As a result of this ancient tale sleep temples became important healing sanctuaries in which the concept of dream incubation first began: where priests and physicians healed a person through dreams that divinely guided them. While in a state of consciousness in the dream (lucid dreaming) seekers called the gods into the dream chamber (*abaton*) and requested a divine healing. Frankincense was burned to invoke the goddess of memory and remembrance, Mnemosyne, in the final stages of dream incubation.

It's unknown exactly how the healing was effective, but when you are in a lucid state (which is similar to hypnosis) your mind and body are more receptive to suggestions. Any dreams or visions would be reported to a priest, who would prescribe the appropriate therapy after interpreting the dreams. Physicians at the temple would also administer herbs and potions to assist in lucid dreaming, much as some shamanic practices use to achieve out-of-body experiences.

What ancient and indigenous traditions have in common is the belief that we are able to heal in the dreaming stage and create a new future for ourselves when we bring the healing back into our waking life, when those lost parts of ourselves are retrieved and returned to completeness. As this involved an external party – the priest, priestess, god, goddess or shaman – we need to work out how to achieve a state of wholeness on our own. Jung suggested that the best way to heal, to integrate the conscious and the unconscious, was through 'individuation'.

Individuation is a lifelong process in which elements of the personality, the immature psyche and a person's life experiences are integrated into a functioning whole.

LIVING YOUR STORY

In our continuous search for knowledge, healing and transformation we each have our own story while at the same time being part of a collective story of humanity. We see ourselves reflected in storytelling; as children we were read stories that made sense of our place in the world. You may not be consciously aware of it, but your life is directed and influenced by the stories you see, hear and read. What story do you tell yourself about who you are? If you allow yourself to be defined by others you will fail to discover who you really are at your very essence.

Cue: enter your dream.

When your dreams call you to awaken to your larger sense of purpose then the little story of who you are will be replaced by a bigger story. Your personal stories connect with the myths of past heroes and heroines, also known as archetypes (see further on this chapter for more information on archetypes).

Courage, resilience and inner strength are required to break the restricted narrative of who you're told you are and embrace your identity as who you want to be. Your dreams ask of you: are you living your bigger story, or are you stuck inside a limited storyline bound tightly by the expectations of others? You'll know if you are living your bigger story, in which you are the hero and not just an extra in the movie, because you vibrate passion and excitement and consciously live in the now. Your big story is mythic because it's larger than your limited version of who you are. It's vital you take notice of the dreams you have with mythical elements.

It will help if you listen to your heart instead of your head when the inner critic and the system tell you who you are and who you should be. You might like to consider asking yourself these questions:

◎ Who am I?

◎ What am I doing in my life?

◎ Where am I going?

◎ How am I being called to become my best possible self?

◎ What might my bigger story look like?

Dreams and myth come from the same place: from finding expression in symbols. Most cultures, from ancient times through to the present, have creation stories that relate how the world came to be. A myth that uses symbolic and metaphoric language to weave the truth in its intricate and poetic sacred narrative.

❖ ACTIVITY PAGE ❖

You are your own dream interpreter and only you
know what your dreams mean, as each symbol
is unique to your experience. Dream symbols will
inevitably spill over into your waking life, and this is
where they manifest as signs and synchronicities.

SYMBOLS, SIGNS AND SYNCHRONICITIES

Symbols that live in your mind have a powerful effect in the energy field. Look at the signs and symbols around you in your everyday waking life, then put questions to the world and see what answers you receive through further signs and symbols. A white feather on your path while you are asking for spiritual guidance might confirm that you are being taken care of. Perhaps you might have been deciding between two options and the Nike sign on the bus says 'Just do it'. Messages also come through music, songs, conversations and books opening just at the right page.

Create your own personal book of signs and symbols. You will gain confidence in understanding your own dream symbols as they reflect those in your conscious world. Remember that reality is encoded with the language of dreams.

Sometimes we are too piled up with social engagements, social media and devices to really notice synchronicities. Spend time writing down your thoughts, emotions and deep reflections; you may wish to draw something that reflects how you are feeling. Disconnect from the noise of daily life: go for a walk in the park, bush or countryside, listen to inspiring music or eat mindfully. Re-ignite your inner imaginal world.

DREAM INCUBATION

- ◎ Imagine how you can manifest and create a future that best sustains you and everyone and everything on this planet. How do you want to feel? Allow yourself the freedom to dream your life into being, remembering that you were made for dreaming for big ideas and for following your passions. Don't hold yourself back; don't give up on your dreams. Put pen to paper and list your dreams.

- ◎ Put on some music, light a candle, make yourself some herbal tea and sit in your favourite spot in the garden or your sacred space at home or somewhere you feel connected to.

- ◎ Don't question or judge your dreams; let your thoughts flow. There are no dreams too small or too big.

- ◎ Bring back a symbol from your night dream: a scene, person, animal or emotion. Weave it into your day dream.

- ◎ Once you bring your dream into consciousness you will find it easier to incubate a dream and receive further guidance.

- ◎ Keep journals for both day and night dreams and share them with others.

NAPPING

To maximise your circadian rhythm, try to have an afternoon nap between 1.30 pm and 3.30 pm. Slipping into a hypnagogic state during this time will induce lucidity and you will experience vivid recall.

EVERY GREAT DREAM BEGINS WITH A DREAMER.

Chapter 5

THE HERO'S JOURNEY

---

*'We must be willing to get rid of
the life we've planned, so as to have
the life that is waiting for us.'*

– JOSEPH CAMPBELL

Joseph Campbell, literature professor and mythologist and author of *The Hero with a Thousand Faces,* studied the myths and legends of various cultures worldwide and noticed a similar, universal storyline he called the 'monomyth' (one myth): in it a hero goes on a quest, meets and is victorious in challenges and returns home transformed. This structure became known as the hero's journey, and Campbell said we are all heroes of our own story. The concept of the hero's journey can be applied to your own life and will help you to understand and overcome the ups and downs of your own journey.

This chapter invites you to step into your shadow as you follow your personal hero's journey – both the inner and outer journey. The waking and dreaming worlds provide you with a bigger story of who you are and what you are capable of becoming.

Note: I use the word 'hero' and 'he' in this chapter, as did Campbell in his original book in 1949; however, it references both heroes and heroines. Also, some readers may be gender fluid or not identify with either the hero or heroine archetype. Let your intuition guide you to select those characteristics that best resonate with you.

> The hero's journey is a process of individuation that involves figuring out who you really are and transforming the vision you have about the world and yourself. Through this process of self-expression of your true nature you have an opportunity for wholeness.

Psychologist and one-time Freud student, Carl Jung, believed there were 12 universal, mythic archetypes with basic motivations within our collective unconscious. He valued dreams highly, believing they were an important part of personality development, and studied how the various archetypes shaped us: the divine child, the great mother, the wise man and old woman, the trickster and, of course, the hero, among others.

Best-selling novels and blockbuster movies with a hero follow the same plot line of the hero's journey. The iconic 1977 *Star Wars* movie is a perfect example of a monomyth and we can all identify with the hero at a psychological level. The main characters from movies such as *The Hunger Games*, the Harry Potter series, *The Matrix*, *The Lion King*, *Mulan*, *The Lord of the Rings* and *Spider Man* follow the hero's path.

Who or what is a hero? Joseph Campbell defines a hero as 'someone who has given his or her life to something bigger than oneself'. The hero is an archetypal figure seen in literature and other art forms throughout history in cultures from all around the world. There are no shortages of heroes, from fables, myths and fairytales to modern superheroes. Some of these figures take amazing journeys that test their heroic strengths and sense of self-worth, while others go through incredible suffering for a greater purpose to become heroic. Superheroes have unnatural strengths they have to balance against monsters and villains.

Archetypes are activated in your dreams during important transitions.

Mythology author Jean Houston said: 'In becoming a Hero or Heroine, we undertake the extraordinary task of dying to our current, local selves and being reborn to our external selves.'

In a typical hero's journey an ordinary person sets off on an adventure to dangerous and dark places where he battles evil, chaos and death. The traveller overcomes obstacles with the help of a mentor who prepares him for even greater challenges. Along the way the traveller must make difficult decisions and face his inner demons. There are rewards in store but the traveller needs to make it back home first, with many temptations along the way to hold him back from finishing his quest. Finally, he returns to his ordinary world a hero, is rewarded and is ultimately transformed.

You may recognise this structure in your own life journey. It is not a once-off journey but is cyclical, continuing throughout your life usually during pivotal stages that require you to get out of your comfort zone. At a deeper level the hero's journey concerns the psyche, with real and symbolic stages along the way that vary depending on your circumstances. It's about finding out who you really are, about your relationships and your view of the world and about transforming your vision as you delve deeper into your subconscious mind. Your dreams hold the clue to your inner search for self-awareness and to finding the courage to express your true nature.

STAGES OF THE HERO'S JOURNEY IN DREAMS

Campbell encouraged everyone to view their own life as a heroic journey. It's not so much about how strong you are, how many resources you have or how well you can achieve. You become a hero when you are willing and courageous enough to venture out into new territory and face the unknown even if you are afraid. If you're currently feeling stressed, overwhelmed, anxious or depressed or dealing with any illness, then your venture into the unknown territory of your condition and the subsequent healing, recovery and then wholeness becomes your hero's journey.

Your dreams, with their symbols and scenarios, will guide you through the stages.

These 12 stages of the hero's journey are life stages you will experience as an adult and repeat throughout your life, each time emerging wiser and more experienced. The motifs, symbols, patterns, nightmares, sequences and recurrence of your dreams reflect your journey while you sleep.

Whether you remember your dreams or not, your dreaming brain processes your life adventure story, the big mythic story that connects you to everyone in the world at a collective unconscious level.

Look at each dream meaning and theme to help you unlock your inner hero's journey. Mine deep for nuggets of self-awareness you can bring back into your waking life so the dream has a transformative effect on you and on those around you.

Below is a diagram of the 12 stages of the hero's journey. Although the stages illustrate the narrative of the journey that is often used in books and movies, I have adapted this information to fit into waking life stages as well as how these stages are experienced through dream images. Additionally, I have included what your psyche is doing during each stage. You will experience subconscious and unconscious emotional growth or blocks during the stages of your life journey.

As you read through each stage of the hero's journey, contemplate how your dream life and waking life have colluded to bring about knowledge and self-awareness during those times you vividly remember being out of your comfort zone.

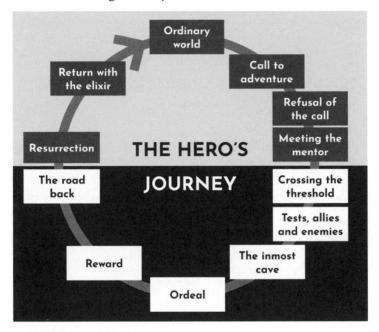

1. ORDINARY WORLD

We meet the hero

This stage is where the hero exists before his big story begins. He's living his little story, his ordinary life, and is totally oblivious of the adventures to come. It's his safe place – predictable and routine – and his everyday life reminds us of our own mundane life. It is business as usual in this ordinary or known world.

Psyche: limited awareness.

In dreams: dreams take place in your ordinary life, whether it's in your house or car or at work. You might ignore them at first because they look identical to your real life and your dreaming mind is not interested, but the longer you are in the dream the more you will notice that it's not exactly the same as your everyday life. This altered reality can only mean your dream is asking you to go with the changes that are about to be revealed.

Common dream themes: your lawn is fluoro green or is moving like water; new rooms are discovered in your house; the foundations of your house are not stable; long corridors that have no end.

2. CALL TO ADVENTURE

The hero begins the journey

The hero's adventure begins when he receives a call to action. This might come as a threat to his own safety or to the safety of others, and might even be a sudden event where he has to step up. The end result is the same: it disrupts his ordinary world and presents a challenge or quest that must be undertaken for the good of all. You may regard this as a call to live a more awakened life. It may be a time in your life when something out of the ordinary happens, something unexpected that you have to deal with.

Psyche: increased self-awareness.

In dreams: you may experience some unpleasant or uncomfortable dream scenes. When you are asked to join an adventure it shakes your foundations and pushes you forcefully out of your comfort zone. In your dreams you will have little or no control. You will likely awake from these out-of control-dreams feeling ungrounded, unnerved or disturbed.

Common dream themes: dream scenes may include shooting; murder; being chased; falling; events occurring in slow motion; dead people; zombies; having a new role that is unfamiliar such as being a boss or of the opposite sex; being in a movie; being trapped; driving a car when the brakes fail.

3. REFUSAL OF THE CALL

The hero refuses to move from his comfort zone

The hero may want to accept the quest but is held back by his fears. He wonders if he is up to the challenge. Insecurity forces him to abandon the call, which consequently causes him to feel conflicted. The problem he faces may seem too much to handle when compared with the comfort of home.

We can all relate to this response from the reluctant hero. Where in your life have you had to put aside the order and structure you have carefully curated against the randomness of life and been obligated or asked to go in a completely different direction? It may be moving jobs, divorce, illness, having to care for a family member or anything that takes you out of your comfort zone and demands you give it your full attention. Think of a time when you've had to make a decision but you were in denial for a while, refusing to acknowledge the change required and hoping it would pass or you minimised the seriousness.

Psyche: resistant to change.

In dreams: your subconscious is making sure you have some memorable anxiety dreams or nightmares so you pay attention. This is no time to be complacent: you are being called to live your bigger life, to go on an adventure to find yourself.

Common dream themes: being stuck, paralysed or unable to move; missing the bus; the brakes on your car not working; turning up to an exam unable to finish it or you don't have the right pen or room and so on; being unable to speak; being buried; being naked in public; being a helpless baby.

4. MEETING THE MENTOR

The hero comes across wisdom

This is a pivotal moment for the hero: he is no longer alone in his thoughts and actions or inaction. He meets a mentor figure who provides guidance and whatever knowledge he needs, and gives him enough confidence and courage to begin the quest.

At times when you need reassurance or good advice the perfect mentor will appear, and you will know immediately if it's the right advice or help. Joseph Campbell said that although everyone has to pass a threshold of some kind we are also protected by destiny or a higher power.

Psyche: overcoming resistance.

In dreams: what a relief it is when a dream magically gives you an ally out of nowhere when you least expect it and you need it the most. Your psyche's message is that there is always a helper – usually that part of your own wiser self – who knows what to do in times of doubt. Trust your inner, wiser voice.

Common dream themes: help from animals that have special powers; spirit guides; possessing supernatural powers; ghosts; holy figures; angels; the dead; snakes; boatman (as in the River Styx); birds.

5. CROSSING THE THRESHOLD

The hero commits to the quest

The hero has now committed to the quest although we don't know what it is: it may be physical, spiritual or emotional. Will he go willingly, or will he be pushed into it? This is the pivotal stage where he crosses the Rubicon; there is no going back. He crosses the threshold between his ordinary, familiar world into one that is in foreign territory. It's one of many firsts for the hero, and when you remember the firsts in your life it may look like the first time you left home or did something new that you thought you would never have the courage to try.

Let the journey into the unfamiliar begin!

Pscyhe: renewed sense of purpose.

In dreams: the adventure truly begins in your dream world as you embark on exciting travel to faraway places. Imagine sailing on a yacht, flying in a hot air balloon, riding a wild horse or driving along a winding coastline: all of these scenarios are preparing you for what is to follow, something that does not presently exist in your ordinary world.

Common dream themes: unfamiliar places; being lost; unusual landscapes that don't make sense; being naked in public; meeting strangers both menacing and friendly; taxis and drivers; authority figures such as police or judges; wizards; flying or sailing.

6. TESTS, ALLIES AND ENEMIES

The hero faces new challenges and obstacles

Now out of his comfort zone, the hero steps into a special world with new challenges that test him. He has to try to overcome each of the obstacles that is placed in his way. Campbell refers to this stage as the belly of the whale, in which the hero faces a series of challenges, temptations and tests uniquely designed for his transformation. Only if the hero survives will he emerge transformed.

The hero needs to work out who to trust. He may find allies and meet enemies who will help prepare him for the more difficult tasks.

Psyche: ready for survival mode.

In dreams: obstacle dreams are the order of the day when you are being tested in some way. The dream is asking if you have the grit to continue on with a difficult decision or task or are you going to give up when the going gets tough? Many frustrating dreams that seem unrelated and surreal will haunt your night-time sleep, with lots of thrashing about in bed before the early morning gives you a reprieve from this parallel dream world.

Common dream themes: being stuck and unable to move; teeth falling out; having to perform feats that are unfamiliar and take superhuman strength or cunning; holding back a fence or door so the assailant doesn't come in; having to scale heights or fly over treacherous waters; swimming with sea creatures and not drowning; islands; going to the toilet with no door; wild animals attacking.

7. THE INMOST CAVE

The hero prepares to get closer to his quest

'The cave you fear to enter holds the treasure you seek.'
– JOSEPH CAMPBELL

The inmost cave is not necessarily a physical place but is where the hero experiences resistance. It is a metaphor for facing your biggest fear and challenge, where there is a danger in confronting your inner conflict. As the hero approaches the cave he must make final preparations before taking a leap into the great unknown. This brief retreat is a cue that there is much more hardship yet to come, and tension is to about to build in anticipation of the ultimate test.

The issue with this stage of the hero's journey is that the hero has no idea how long he's going to be inside the whale, whether the whale will spit him out or if he has to force the whale to release him or perhaps a supernatural helper will rescue him. Nothing is certain when the hero approaches his inmost cave, which is why there is resistance to go there.

Psyche: preparing for greater uncertainties.

In dreams: despair, loneliness and loss are the big emotions that dominate this part of your journey. The dream will reveal you at your most vulnerable, when you are separated or abandoned by everyone or everything you know. It reflects the waking life call to separate from the noise of the world, from social media and from expectations and get out of the rat race to think through clearly where you want to go and who you want to become. This is unknown and uncomfortable territory.

If you have begun your hero's journey and are feeling a little stuck or are uncertain in what direction to go next it is most likely you are in the belly of the whale stage. Have no doubt about it: you are being prepared for major growth ahead. After you're reborn you have to grow up. Your dreams will be dark and emotional and make no sense in the dream sequence. Know that you are experiencing a dark night of the soul: a catharsis, or simply being like a caterpillar in a cocoon waiting for the right time to emerge as a butterfly and fly away.

Common dream themes: separation and loss; death; being killed or murdered; losing your teeth; being in an underground tunnel or cave; being trapped in a mine or a railway tunnel.

8. ORDEAL

The hero faces his biggest fear

'Here we undergo a truly Heroic transformation of consciousness
. . . Either by the trials themselves or by illuminating revelations.
Trials and revelations are what it's all about.'

– JOSEPH CAMPBELL

The hero hits rock bottom. This is the hero's darkest hour, when he confronts his greatest fear: either a series of physical tests or a deep inner crisis. If the hero survives he will emerge transformed, but to do this he must use all of his skills and the experiences gathered from the inmost cave to overcome his most difficult challenge yet.

To be reborn the hero must release some part of himself; only then can he gain greater insight into how to reach his ultimate goal. Will he survive this 'death'?

Psyche: confronting and letting go of the fear of death as a catalyst for change.

In dreams: in most journeys the hero will face death many times, so there will be a series of dreams sequences that will have a death theme. Death in dreams is not a literal death in waking life, but it is an ending of some kind: the ending of an old behaviour pattern, way of life, job role that no longer fits or relationship that no longer works. It's always painful to kill off all that is familiar. Change is hard, even when it's good.

Where there is an ending there is a beginning. No matter how challenging it is to end the past status quo, all the lessons learned from an experience build character: all the strength, courage, resilience and maturity can be retained and brought into the new.

You may wake during the night with nightmares caused by your traumas, emotional triggers and painful memories, but like a butterfly emerging from the chrysalis you'll gain new awareness and abilities.

As the hero, you will emerge from the dark night of the soul transformed, but first you must endure sitting with the discomfort, the fear and the nightmares.

Common dream themes: being in a plane or car crash; giving birth to a deformed child or animal; dead bodies; losing a limb; being in a burning house or watching it burn; being attacked and mauled by a wild animal; a violent encounter with a ghostly figure at the end of your bed; lost in a forest all alone; wrestling a lion.

9. REWARD

The hero seizes the sword and feels hopeful

The hard work pays off when the hero defeats the enemy, survives and is ready to continue to the next part of the journey. He has become stronger for his suffering and has been rewarded for it but, whatever the treasure or personal victory, he is not yet ready to celebrate. There is still a distance to go before the journey ends.

Psyche: accepting of consequences.

In dreams: dreams of being the opposite gender reflect the transformation that has taken place at an emotional level. The hero has integrated both his masculine action side and his feminine intuitive side and can enjoy the fruits of his labour. It's common to dream of either making love to someone of the same gender or yourself being of the opposite gender when you have done a fair bit of self-development. You've come to understand your inner conflicts and have learned to balance your yin and yang.

Carl Jung believed that women have a masculine (animus) unconscious side to their psyche and men a feminine (anima) unconscious side. When someone has achieved a union of the two sides in their inner world they then reach a balanced state. Jung also believed the animus and anima were essential for the journey towards individuation, transforming an unformed person into a unique individual.

Common dream themes: finding or being given a set of keys; crossing a bridge; being in an unknown landscape; running in a race; rescuing a child or animal; swords; eating fruit; riding a horse; being the opposite gender.

10. THE ROAD BACK

The hero's journey home is longer than expected

The hero has to journey back home to the ordinary world with his reward but his journey is not yet over. However, now there are more dangers than before as his reward may have angered the dragon whose treasure he stole or an opposing army is waiting to ambush him to reclaim what they feel is owed to the kingdom.

It's not time for the hero to relax just yet; he may even give himself up. Can the hero commit to the last stage of his journey? How will he choose between his own personal goal and that of a higher cause?

'At the darkest moment comes the light.'

– JOSEPH CAMPBELL

Psyche: recommit to the original purpose of the quest.

In dreams: the conflict between your self-interests and those that are for the greater good creates interesting dream images. You want to be the master of your own destiny yet something else is driving you to become what you had never imagined.

Attics represent your higher self or spiritual side while basements symbolise the subconscious, the hidden parts of you that want to remain undisturbed. Is the controlling force benevolent, or is it simply a matter of duty, obligation, guilt, pride or glory seeking? This is the stage in your life when you have to search deeply into your soul to find some answers.

Common dream themes: attics and basements; graves; churches; witches; road trips; ships or boats; mountains; caves.

11. RESURRECTION

The hero's final attempt to complete his quest

This is the climax of the story, the final test for the hero and his most dangerous battle with death. The dark side is given yet another opportunity to decimate the hero, and the stakes are high. This one additional resurrection, having been tested through the ordeal, is really the final battle. The outcome will affect all those he left behind in the ordinary world. The hero feels afraid but ultimately succeeds, destroying the enemy and emerging from battle victorious and reborn as a true hero.

Psyche: being open to a final breakthrough.

In dreams: water dreams should always alert you to your emotional state. Emerging from one state to another, from an embryo into a baby for example, represents the enormity of your growth and potential. Like the hero you have been reborn and in a way baptised into a new way of being, a new community of heroes. Images in dreams consist of flying, denoting control and victory and going up in an elevator (an elevation of status).

At this stage of your life you may have won the battle but not necessarily the war. You have scars to prove your bravery, but there will come a time when you may have to face more challenges and go on another journey.

Common dream themes: water; babies; fish; tunnels; elevators; fire; flying.

12. RETURN WITH THE ELIXIR

The hero returns home in triumph

The hero finally returns home, but is not the same person he was when he left his ordinary world and set off on the journey. He will have grown and matured and be looking forward to the start of a new life.

The elixir he brings back to help others may be literal or metaphoric, such as a new invention or simply hope. It symbolises all that the hero has learned along the way, and now it's time to give back and be of service to others.

The hero's outgrown his old self. He is forever changed and nothing will ever be same again. This is the end of one cycle and the beginning of a new one. The psyche is ready to take another journey and peel off another layer of the hero's self.

Psyche: life in review.

In dreams: if you revisit a place where you previously lived you may be struck by how much has changed or not changed; you will see things from a new perspective. You may meet some people you used to know who will tell you how much you've changed. Everything is the same and nothing is the same.

After following the hero's journey and reaching the end you come full circle and are back at the beginning. When you come up against an issue you've worked on and thought you'd resolved you may be stunned that you have to go through the experience again. This is the part of the hero's journey where you bring the elixir back to yourself: you have faced the threat and won, and now you can utilise the wisdom you've acquired to help you this time around.

Common dream themes: lost in an unknown landscape; riding into the unknown; driving on an unfamiliar road; losing your passport; seeing yourself as an old man or woman.

LESSONS FROM THE HERO'S JOURNEY

Whenever dreams bring up discomfort and confusion, be aware that you are somewhere on the hero's journey. When life and dreams intersect and you are reluctant to heed the call, you have the choice to either embark on your quest or remain where you are. Bear in mind that a limited life is a wasted life and a much lonelier one than an adventurous life that is uniquely yours. Where to now?

> You can choose to view trials and obstacles as part of your quest and create meaning and purpose around them, or remain resistant to change and never experience the adventure of inner work and individuation.

Heeding the call is an opportunity to face your fears, whether in real life or in dreams. Let your dreams guide you and inspire you to live a bigger, mythic life.

THE MAJOR ARCANA OF THE TAROT AND THE FOOL'S JOURNEY

The tarot is more than a fortune-telling device: the cards represent a cosmic model of the universe filled with human experience, revealing patterns of past, present and probable future. It uses archetypal symbolism, elemental meaning, mysticism, astrology and numerology. A tarot deck is usually made up of 78 cards divided into two separate arcana (Latin for 'secrets' or 'mysteries'). The Major Arcana consists of 22 cards, while the remaining 56 comprise the Minor Arcana.

Both the journey and the characters in the tarot are universally encountered in dreams, each one symbolising an aspect of actual figures or qualities and features in your life. The Major Arcana of the tarot uses The Fool as the key figure representing the human journey and the figures encountered throughout your life. The hero's journey closely parallels the rites of passage of The Fool's journey; both are based on archetypal experience. Although The Fool is represented as a male due to the traditional stereotype of the time the cards were created, there is no specific gender assigned. In your dreams you can see yourself playing the archetypal part of The Fool in whatever way your psyche wants you to see.

You must begin by first defining your own journey of identity:

- ◎ Who are you?

- ◎ What do you stand for?

- ◎ What parts of yourself are hidden, rejected or ignored?

- ◎ How can you integrate all of these parts to achieve wholeness?

- ◎ Are you the best person you can be; is this the best version of yourself?

Each of the 22 cards in the Major Arcana embodies an archetypal figure and symbolises the various stages of The Fool's (your own) journey and how you must integrate all parts of yourself as you are led to wholeness.

0. The Fool is a carefree and happy wanderer, innocent and unaware of taking the dangerous journey of life ahead. He is known as a fool because he has the innocent faith to undertake such as journey, representing each of us as a naive traveller through life on a grand adventure and taking a leap of faith.

1. The Magician, the first character The Fool encounters, is dynamic masculine energy, a skilled and masterful alchemist who is in control of his own life.

2. The High Priestess is the mysterious keeper of spiritual secrets. Guarded and secretive, she embodies the elements of femininity and intuition. The Fool has met both his masculine and feminine aspects.

3. The Empress is the archetypal mother: nurturing, abundant and loving. She is the feminine provider who feeds and protects all of her creation. The Fool feels nourished and safe.

4. The Emperor holds the energy of the father, the protector and provider who rules and creates order from chaos in the world. The Fool is being instilled with knowledge on boundaries and rules by the parental figures of The Empress and The Emperor.

5. The Hierophant is a symbol of dogma, hierarchy and authority who passes down knowledge through the lens of religious and cultural institutions. The Fool begins his formal education.

6. The Lovers represent the principles of opposition and attraction, the choice between two equally strong desires. The Fool must take his knowledge to the world. He yearns for a loving relationship but he first needs to decide upon his beliefs. The future is in his hands.

7. The Chariot represents forward movement and progress. The Fool has developed inner control through discipline and will power.

8. Strength is represented by a woman with the heart of a lion. The Fool learns that the gentler power of loving approach is sometimes better than the wilful command of The Chariot.

9. The Hermit is a recluse who is removed from the usual frantic activity of life and represents the need to find a deeper truth. The Fool begins to look inward and spends time in solitude.

10. The Wheel of Fortune is the spinning wheel of fate and destiny. Life is a series of twists and turns influenced by both choice and fate; The Fool has to accept fortune's unpredictable changes.

11. Justice is the maker and enforcer of laws by which The Fool must trace the cause and effect relationships have brought him to this point.

12. The Hanged Man is suspended in time, sacrificing his passions for a better outcome and future. The Fool has to learn to relinquish his struggle for control in order to find joy.

13. Death is the card of transition and endings. The Fool eliminates old habits and clears away beliefs he's outgrown to allow the growth of the new. He is forever changed by his experiences.

14. Temperance is represented by the angel of balance. The Fool needs the moderation and balance of temperance's emotional stability.

15. The Devil is our shadow side, the unconscious urges of the psyche that manifest as addictions. The Fool feels manipulated and hopeless under the seduction of hedonistic passions and desires.

16. The Tower represents sudden release and forceful clearing of heavy energy filled with shock and awe. The lightning bolt shakes The Fool's inner foundations, allowing for new growth and renewal.

17. The Star is our shining light in the dark. The Fool is suffused with calm after the storm and is now filled with inspiration, hope and guidance.

18. The Moon is the symbol of the unconscious mind and the imagination. In this dreamy landscape The Fool is susceptible to fantasy and illusions that cause him to feel confused.

19. The Sun is at the centre of the universe and is a source of life on earth. The Fool receives the gift of vibrancy and assurance so that he is able to realise his greatness.

20. Judgement is a reminder of the power of forgiveness. The Fool has been reborn and his ego self shed as he is absolved of his past mistakes.

21. The World is the card of completion and success, the opportunity to begin again. The Fool re-enters the world with full understanding in which he has integrated all the neglected parts of himself and achieved wholeness. The future is filled with infinite possibilities. The cycle is over but The Fool will not stop growing through his experiences. The pursuit of self-awareness is a continuous practice for life.

YOUR SHADOW SELF: THE DARK SIDE OF DREAMING

In the hero's journey the most frightening part of the ordeal was being inside the belly of a whale. However, it was in getting through this ordeal that the hero emerged as changed forever and new. In The Fool's journey, The Devil created the most fear in the struggle to overcome the darkness or the shadow self. Dreams reflecting this fear are typically your scary dreams and nightmares.

It's normal to feel overwhelmed both in your dream and after waking. It might affect you for a day or even a week because you identify strongly with the role you play in the dream. You remember what it felt like to be the victim being chased? The chaser – menacing, threatening and with no apparent good reason to be chasing you – is the shadow. Even though the threat is begging you to pay attention, rather than focusing on what it represents, you will tend instead to focus on the part you play of the victim running away.

The 'shadow', an idea explored by Carl Jung, is everything in us that is unconscious, repressed, undeveloped and denied. These are dark, rejected aspects of our being but in them is undeveloped potential – the light aspects of ourselves – that is dying to come out. We don't know that our personal shadow has this undeveloped side because it's hidden from us in our unconsciousness. Robert Bly called the shadow self the long black bag we drag behind us that is filled with all our unacceptable qualities. It's a sad image, and you can almost feel the weight of that drag preventing you moving at a natural pace.

We learned as children about things that were acceptable and we identified with them. Whatever was not acceptable we disowned, or put inside the long black bag: when we were told not to be a sissy we didn't cry; when we spoke confidently we were told we had too much personality; when we were imaginative we were told to be practical. And so we hid these parts: we kept being expressive, assertive and visionary in the shadows because these attributes were deemed to be undesirable or unacceptable.

In the unconscious the shadow qualities gain in strength and momentum, and in time of stress they burst out and you project them onto others, which causes tension and dissonance with the people around you. However, in the dream world these qualities are insidious.

When something is avoided, rejected or pushed away it doesn't actually disappear but goes underground, into the unconscious, where it gains in strength and power. If you don't meet them in your dreams they manifest as anxiety, anger, depression and illness or accidents in your waking life.

In dreams the shadow commonly appears as an indistinct figure that may take on other appearances such as a zombie or walking dead; a ghoul; a dark shape; someone or something you feel uneasy about or are repelled by; anything dark or threatening; any aggressor; a devil; a monster; an intimidating animal; a catastrophic event such as a tsunami; someone you know who is younger than you such as a sibling or work colleague; a foreigner; a servant; a prostitute; a burglar.

It's difficult to recognise the shadow as it often takes the form of someone of the same gender as you, the dreamer, someone who has qualities you don't like or that irritate you. Confusingly, it may also be someone with qualities you admire, qualities you have not yet achieved in yourself: your undeveloped potential. Sometimes you can't even see what the shadow is, but you can feel it's there as a dark energy and you are wary of it.

So how do you meet your shadow in your dreams instead of running away?

The classical chase dream is the most common dream we all share universally; everyone has had this dream and remembered it at least once in their lifetime.

External triggers can range from seeing someone who looks like a person who hurt you in the past in some way or attending an event such as a birthday party or work or anniversary celebration that brings up emotions related to a significant time and/or trauma in your life. These triggers from the waking world will usually result in encountering the shadow in your dreams, and there is only one way to work with this dream image: to turn towards it. You may even be brave enough to confront it boldly and ask it what it wants.

If you found out what the shadow wanted from you, no matter how ambiguous, repulsive or frightening it was, you could be kind and gracious enough to give your time. It's the same principle as in the fairytale of *Beauty and the Beast:* love or accept the shadow and it will transform into a positive force.

As in the hero's journey, once you accept the call to adventure and leave the ordinary, waking world you have no option but to go in the dream world to your inmost cave, face and conquer the ordeal and come out the other side changed for having gone through the process. Facing the shadow is pivotal to coming back to the ordinary world with an elixir of hope and change. The cycle is complete. The next stage of the journey to self-awareness is complete.

FACING YOUR SHADOW

There are no bad dreams, because all dreams offer helpful insights into what is affecting you. They shine a light on those rejected, denied or forgotten parts of you that are ready to come to consciousness in the process known as enlightenment. If you are experiencing recurring dreams, the more you ignore them the louder the bad dreams will get and they could turn into full-blown nightmares. In time they may manifest in waking life as anger, depression or even illness. Ideally, meeting the dark, scary figures in your dreams head on instead of running away from them will increase your courage. In waking life it means you are able to live with your imperfections, failings, disappointments, anger or grief.

Let's say in a dream you are being chased by a threatening dark figure. You can feel its breath on you as it gets closer; you run, but you're no match for it. You try to scream, but it's that terrifying, choking, silent scream that can't be released from your throat. You know that whatever is chasing you may potentially kill you and are terrified for your life. But what if you stopped running and turned to face the figure? By confronting whatever it is that terrifies you, the cycle of being chased will be broken. Once you see what or who the figure is, ask them what it is that they want from you.

I used to dream of a big sinister black dog chasing me, one that reminded me of the dog in the Arthur Conan Doyle story *The Hound of the Baskervilles*. I could hear its snarling and feel sprays of drool on my back, and was aware it was travelling in a pack! Interestingly, when I researched myths for my oracle deck *Mists of Avalon Oracle*, I found the king of the underworld, Gwyn ap Nudd, was depicted as having his red-eyed hellish hounds with him as he roamed the world looking for souls to take to the land of the dead.

Imagine if a black dog were to lunge and dig its teeth into your arm: you'd expect it to hurt you but would find that in actual fact it didn't hurt at all. You are surprised, but you also feel a sense of rapport with the dog. The bite was intended not to hurt you, but to be recognised by you. At the point of the bite making contact with your arm, you reconnected with some disowned part of yourself. You could ask yourself if you have been loyal to your pack (your instincts) or whether you have been neglecting your instincts for some time. Did it take a bite from a hound to remind you of your disconnection from yourself? Why had you been running away from your instincts in the first place?

Keeping a dream journal is an ideal practice for this type of dream.

> When you experience recurring dream themes and images it reflects a recurring pattern in your life that keeps you from moving forward.

Use coloured codes to do an analysis and see which of your dreams share similar themes. Date the dream entries so you can trace back what was happening at that time in your life.

By integrating both your shadow and light aspects you will begin on the journey to becoming whole. Your hero's journey will be done for now when you let something go, something that no longer serves you. This can feel like you are in a dark place because it's unknown territory that hasn't been explored before. This is your underworld.

DREAMS AND THE UNDERWORLD

The Greek goddess Persephone was able to live in both the underworld and on earth. She was the daughter of Demeter (goddess of the harvest) and Zeus (king of the gods) who then became the wife of Hades (king of the underworld) and therefore the queen of the underworld after integrating both parts of her psyche: the dark and rejected side and her positive traits. We discover that these traits are equally essential for growth and consciousness.

According to myth, Persephone was gathering flowers when she was abducted by the dark king of the underworld, Hades. Demeter was so angry after searching everywhere for her daughter she went into a long period of grieving, losing interest in the harvest and fertility of the earth which subsequently resulted in widespread famine.

The sacred crone Hecate found out where Persephone was being held and asked for Zeus to intervene, demanding that Hades release Persephone to her mother. That proved to be difficult, however, because Persephone had eaten a pomegranate seed in the underworld and, because of this, was bound to Hades. She could not be completely freed but had to remain in the underworld, the land of the dead, in winter and part of autumn, only being able to return to her mother in the land of the living in spring and summer. Persephone became a compassionate and wise queen of the underworld. She had become lost in darkness but eventually found her way through.

Like Persephone, there are times when you will be plunged into the dark, held captive by your deepest or unknown fears. But it's in the dark that you come face to face with your fears and have the opportunity to reclaim those unwanted or unknown parts of yourself you've lost.

The shadow or repressed parts remain unconscious and cause you to act in ways that bring conflict in your waking life, or they may represent your unlived life. When you bring them into awareness and integrate them you can live a more balanced and conscious life. Persephone represents both the light and the shadow aspects of ourselves as she is both innocence, when she surfaces in springtime, and the experience she brings from the depths of the underworld.

On the path to transformation, as on the hero's journey, you reach a point where you either break down or you break through, and it often happens that the breakdown comes before the breakthrough.

You are connected to the myth of Persephone because, like the hero, she represents the journey of transformation from innocence to wisdom; from unconscious to conscious; from fear to ruling over your own inner kingdom.

❖ ACTIVITY PAGE ❖

SHADOW WORK

Choose a dream in which there is a shadow figure. Describe them exactly as you remember them – what they looked, sounded and felt like – and the details of what happened in the dream.

◎ List (a) the threat, (b) what you did to save yourself and (c) how successful or unsuccessful you were.

◎ After reading the section on the shadow self, work out what the chase dream was trying to show you about the neglected parts of yourself. If there was no chase involved, how did you feel when you were attacked by the shadow? Write this down.

◎ Rewrite the dream with a new perspective: what if it was just an initiation? What if you had to prove yourself worthy by being courageous in the face of terror and suffering? Would you see your nightmares and the shadow as totally negative? What would the shadow have to say to you if you just stopped and listened? Notice any recurring patterns in your dreams so you can work out how your shadow characters and images become integrated.

◎ When you experience a journey from the darkness of a current challenge to the light and power of your new transformed self you are connected to Persephone. Create a vision board with gifts that can be mined underground and brought back from the darkness into light and consciousness.

◎ Write in your journal what part of your life you may be ready to rebirth. Break it up in these sections: release from the old; crossing the threshold; bringing something new to your life.

THE HERO'S JOURNEY JOURNAL

If you have a kept a dream journal, go back and see which stages of the hero's journey your dreams related to. Create your own hero's journey chart and put the 12 stages into your own words. Begin with 'a call to life' instead of 'a call to adventure'. Before bedtime, review your structure and ask your dreams to guide you and show you how to overcome any part of the structure that needs attention.

Look at these sayings and list those ones that resonate best with your own dreams. Rewrite what your life might look like if you could enact any of these mantras:

◎ live the dream

◎ dream without limitations

◎ dreams come true

◎ dream big

◎ dream as if anything is possible

◎ every great dream begins with a dreamer

◎ I have the power to dream and do

◎ dream it, live it, be it.

MAJOR ARCANA VISUALISATION

In the following exercise, you will experience altered consciousness, which is what your active dreaming mind does. It will make you more aware of your intuition and allow you to connect with the collective unconscious and universal patterns (archetypes) at a deeper level:

- Sit somewhere private and quiet, play some quiet background music and light a candle. Relax and breathe gently and deeply.

- Lay your Major Arcana cards on a flat surface. Think of one archetypal feature you want to have more of – courage, compassion, wisdom, fairness – and link it to one of the archetypes represented in the tarot. See which card your subconscious mind chooses; it may not be what your conscious mind would choose.

- Stare at the card until your eyes are almost blurry. Don't move your eyes: focus on one part of the card only. This is known as a self-induced trance. Don't think of anything, just allow the image to seep into your mind without judgement. Empty your mind of all thoughts.

- Say out loud the archetype personality trait you wish to embody, for example, courage.

- Keep staring at the card and let the word swirl in your mind as you continue to focus. Count to five, then blink and look at the card from further away.

- Come back into the present, back into room.

DREAM
AS
IF
ANYTHING
IS
POSSIBLE.

Chapter 6

LUCID DREAMING

'Once upon a time, I dreamt I was a butterfly, fluttering hither and thither, to all intents and purposes a butterfly. I was conscious only of my happiness as a butterfly, unaware that I was myself. Soon I awaked, and there I was, veritably myself again. Now I do not know whether I was then a man dreaming I was a butterfly, or whether I am now a butterfly, dreaming I am a man.'

– ZHUANGZI, THE BUTTERFLY AS COMPANION: MEDITATIONS ON THE FIRST THREE CHAPTERS OF THE CHUANG-TZU

As you journey into lucid dreaming you traverse unknown territory: a foreign country with unfamiliar landscapes and inhabitants who may surprise you with their hospitality or shock you with their hostility. As a consciousness traveller you must take a leap of faith into this new world where you are awake within your dreamscape.

WHAT IS LUCID DREAMING?

You are lucid or conscious dreaming when you know you are dreaming while you are in a dream; *lucid* means you are clear and possess full consciousness. You know if you've had a lucid dream because it's so real it feels more real than your waking life. It's unforgettable and it can hook you into wanting to experience more.

The seduction of a lucid dream is that it offers unlimited possibilities, allowing you, the dreamer, to alter the direction of your dreamscape and the events and characters in your dreams. With practice you can control the action like a movie director, increasing parts of your lucid dream world – from living out your fantasy to time travel to meeting guides and other-worldly figures to flying through walls and space.

Lucid dreaming has been enjoying huge popularity, particularly with younger people, who find it relatively easy to enter a lucid dream state and access their creative imagination as they co-create their dream. These young dreamers also have access to hundreds of books, online resources, social media groups and blogs, which give them a huge selection of material and courses from which to choose.

It appears that younger people are well practised at virtual reality through their gaming, which makes it easier for them to enter the vivid world of lucid dreaming. Their brains are familiar with avatars and their function in an alien world. Note, though, that there are many lucid dreamers out there of all ages who have practised lucid dreaming for many years and continue to enjoy the lucid adventures.

This chapter caters mostly for beginner lucid dreamers with recommended reading material at the end of the book for further information and a deeper dive into this fascinating topic.

Not everyone experiences lucid dreaming consistently: some people don't ever experience it while others are born naturals, but most will experience at least one naturally occurring lucid dream in their lifetime. In some lucid dreams the dreamer is ripped away from the dream and back into reality with a sudden jolt; in these cases at least the dreamer gets a glimpse of a vivid reality dream. Other dreamers' experiences are intoxicated with the sense of freedom and control their dreams offer.

The important thing for tackling lucid dreaming is to be disciplined and work with your regular dreams and practise often. If you become good at dream recall it's so much easier to challenge yourself with lucid dreaming. The word 'control' is sometimes misused when describing lucid dreams as being able to 'control' them. When you become lucid in a dream, it's important to remember not to force the events in the dream in order to alter it, which will take away from the natural unconscious state in which the dream message is trying to communicate with you. Unlike a virtual reality game, the purpose of lucid dreaming is not to achieve anything but to engage with the images and scenes in the dream.

In the 1980s, psychophysiologist Stephen LaBerge was responsible for proving to the scientific community that lucid dreaming is possible. It was a breakthrough for the dreaming community, which had no scientific framework for understanding their lucid dreaming mind. Science was able to explain that when we fall asleep we have physical inhibitors that paralyse our bodies so we don't act out our dreams. Using a set of pre-arranged signals of rapid eye movement (REM) on lucid dreaming subjects in his sleep lab, LaBerge communicated with dreamers while they were dreaming. Laboratories worldwide are currently conducting further research into lucid dreaming.

Lucid dreaming is not a new fad. Prior to it being claimed by science as a worthy phenomena to study it had been used by ancient peoples in their spiritual practices. Buddhists use the lucid state in dream yoga for 'dying consciously', that is, becoming awake in their dreams and subsequently in their afterlife. In Shamanism, dreaming can be accessed through other gates such as vision quests, sacred plants (entheogens, or substances that induce alterations in consciousness and behaviour), sweat lodges, purge practice and drumming.

Over my dreaming life I have experienced several lucid dreams by using special techniques such as the candle technique and mnemonic induction of lucid dreams, which is explained later in the chapter. I am not a natural lucid dreamer, but I have entered the liminal space where lucid dreaming presents through various access points. Most importantly, it has become my practice to incubate dreams, to remember dreams and record them in my journal the moment I wake up. I then share them with others so the dream is given life in the waking world outside the confines of the subconscious. If you feel and value the dreaming practice, lucid dreaming can be achieved. According to a recent review study, 55 per cent of adults have experienced at least one lucid dream and 23 per cent experience lucid dreams regularly (once a month or more).

THE ESSENTIALS FOR LUCID DREAMING

Best-selling author and renowned dream expert Robert Waggoner has studied dreams for over 40 years and in particular more than 1,000 lucid dreams. I asked him what the three essential points of lucid dreaming were. These were his responses.

1. *Since lucid dreaming is scientifically validated, it offers us a new way to explore and experiment within the dream state to understand it better. Lucid dreamers from around the world agree on many of the experiential aspects of lucid dreaming, which suggests that the dream state is a principled realm and not chaos or meaningless.*

As someone who spends a lot of time studying, researching and experiencing dreams I find it perplexing when I hear people say 'It's just a dream'. It devalues the dream state itself as well as ancient, indigenous, shamanic and now scientific study because it goes against current cultural thinking and ancient wisdom practices. Those who are interested dreamers will begin to see value in dream-state possibilities, in lucid, out-of-body experiences and other realms of experiential reality as being equally valid as the waking life experience.

2. *Neurologists have called lucid dreaming a 'hybrid state of consciousness' [Ursula Voss, et al., 2012] since the cerebral cortex and other ancient parts of the brain show activation in lucid*

dreaming. The activation of the cerebral cortex indicates that the lucid dreamer is actively making decisions within the lucid dream, considering options, and has a sense of self influence within the dream. While many people consider lucid dreaming to mean 'control', it seems better to state that the lucid dreamer can influence the dream, since he or she must still interact with unconscious material (e.g. dream figures, dream settings, surprising situations) within the lucid dream. Neurologically, the hybrid state of consciousness also suggests this fact.

Lucid dreaming is a fascinating subject for scientific study. As a non-scientist, I will try to explain the workings of a lucid dream simply. When you sleep, your prefrontal cortex, the part of the brain responsible for logic and critical thinking, is dormant as it needs a well-earned rest from the day's busy brain activity. Neurotransmitters, the chemicals that allow for communication between different parts of the brain, are reduced. When you enter REM sleep your body locks up into what is known as sleep paralysis (for further information see page 188), which keeps you motionless while you are in REM so you don't act out your dream.

Lucid dreaming usually takes place in REM sleep, so the more you sleep the more time is spent in REM and the more likely it is that you will have a lucid dream.

The act of dreaming itself happens throughout the brain even though your prefrontal cortex is dormant, but when you lucid dream you bring it back online temporarily. You may notice something is not quite right during a dream – a talking pony, an upside down house, a loved one who has passed away but living life normally – which will get your attention. Once you become lucid the visual part of your brain creates a reality in the same way it does when you are awake; the brain can't tell the difference between dream and reality. By using your awareness you can bring your prefrontal cortex fully online and have a waking experience in the dream. Then you will know you are lucid dreaming.

The following very strange but unbelievably profound dream experience, which was shared with me by an experienced lucid dreamer, is an example of influencing a lucid dream but not having control in how the dream manifests in reality (note: it's not for the faint hearted):

I had a dream repeat three to four times almost identically in a month about a snake on my parents property and it was in the third dream that I became lucid and aware that it was a warning. It was after the second dream of the huge snake slithering at super speed toward my parents house across the grassy area in their yard on the farm I knew I had to tell my mother. As usual, my mother dismissed my dream.

I visited the following week, and that night while sleeping at my parents' house I dreamed there was a huge snake in my room and I locked it in the bedroom closet where I was sleeping. I again told my mum I had dreamed of a snake yet it was in her house this time. I emphasised this was definitely a warning as I had now seen it three times in my dreams and that it was looming close to her house on the farm.

I returned to the city and that evening I had the same dream as the first two dreams, with the huge snake coming toward my mother across the grass from the paddock. I felt present in spirit yet did not see or feel myself in bodily form in my dream. I decided in that moment in my dream that I was going to protect her from the snake. I used my consciousness and harnessed all my spirit power in the dream landscape. I felt as if I was a shield of light and put up a force field so the snake couldn't get fully across the grass area to the house.

I telepathically told/directed the snake to get out of here and thrust energy like wind to the left and the snake was thrust in that direction into the bushes. I awoke in shock again in the middle of the night yet instantly realised that I had changed the dream scenario and it didn't get to the house or to my mum.

My mother called me three days later with news of a snake that came across the grass toward her and the house. She proceeded to explain to me that it was huge, over six feet long, and coming straight at her. She said she worried and was scared as she knew she couldn't move fast enough to get away because the speed of this gigantic brown snake was unbelievable. She then told me: 'You wouldn't believe it, it came racing across the grass and then when three-quarters the way it suddenly took a sharp turn and went flying into the bushes. Never seen anything like it.' That was my dream! In that moment, in my heart and soul and in my mind, was my confirmation that I had been able to change the possible potential of this massive snake getting my mum. I knew innately after the lucid dream and energetically throwing/ thrusting the snake away that it had changed and the threat and warning had been changed.

Not only was this dream redirected in the lucid dream state, but as rare as these kinds of dreams are it was able to change a future event. Keep this in mind when reading information in this book about déjà vu and time constructs (see pages 102 and 262). This also applies to when you are having a nightmare and you change the sequence and ending to a favourable one.

The final point Robert Waggoner made about important keys to lucid dreaming is that it can be used to resolve issues, expand inner awareness and, as the snake dream demonstrates, perform extraordinary feats that result in a positive, healing outcome:

3. Because the lucid dreamer has the capacity to relate consciously to unconscious dream material and also direct themselves within the lucid dream, he or she can use this state for resolving inner issues such as nightmares, phobias, anxiety and so on. Moreover, lucid dreaming may ultimately give scientists insights into the unconscious, which makes waking therapeutic techniques more effective and powerful. The possible benefits of lucid dreaming seem extraordinary.

Some spiritual traditions have said that an action performed at the level of a lucid dream is seven times more powerful than an action performed at the waking level. This idea recognises the influence that can be achieved when you bring your conscious awareness into the dream state.

In my experience, lucid dreamers have used lucid dreaming to enhance their mental and physical health, access inner creativity, relate to an inner awareness and perform spiritual practices. Lucid dreaming serves as an open platform for personal growth when used thoughtfully.

What excites me the most about dreaming in general, but even more about stretching ourselves to lucid dreaming, out-of-body experiences and astral projections, is the fact that we are not ignoring, neglecting or disregarding the one-third of our lives we spend sleeping.

Out of that approximate 25 years we are in a dreaming state for around six years. Imagine the knowledge, experiences and adventures that can be accumulated in that time!

Thinking about my personal experience and examples such as the snake dream makes me question why we lucid dream and why we experience fascinating dreams that seem to take us out of our body?

Meditating or simply being present in a lucid dream and asking to be taken to a place of healing is something everyone has access to. Lucid dream author and researcher Dr Clare Johnson describes lucid dreaming as where 'everything falls away in this healing and nourishing state'. She explains how you can have a non-dual experience in which you release yourself of your body and ego and are given a sense of support. Non-duality is a spiritual term that refers to a mature state of consciousness where the ego or the 'I' is transcended. Not only is this state of healing consciousness available in sleeping, it is also available in the hypnagogic state when you are meditating. It's well documented that this state can help with mental and physical health.

THE BENEFITS OF LUCID DREAMING

| The benefits of lucid dreaming are very appealing and exciting.

It's a break from the predictable reality of life. You become an oneironaut, or an explorer of dreams, in the lucid plane. You can opt for an exhilarating experience where the dream world can be the ultimate virtual reality, allowing you to create and do whatever it is your imagination can handle. The list is infinite, but the fun activities include walking through walls, flying, travelling through space, creating your own world and having special superpowers. Engaging in sexual fantasy while lucid dreaming is extremely common: many people fantasise about having sex with their favourite celebrity or simply being uninhibited. Overall, it's a personal journey into an adventure land without risk of danger.

It is good for resolving emotional trauma, fears, phobias, anxieties and psychological problems. Lucid dreaming is now being used to treat post-traumatic stress disorders. In your lucid dreaming you can recreate the fear and re-script the dream sequence so that you overcome your obstacles and face your fears (see below on how it helps with nightmares).

It improves sport skills and overall confidence. The vivid imagery during lucid dreaming and REM sleep is ideal for establishing a neural pathway in which the body is still but the mind is active. Successful sports people use visualisation techniques to become more proficient and physically stronger. Lucid dreaming has the same purpose. It is useful if you want to prepare for a job interview or presentation that might result in a promotion, or in any situation where you need to build confidence.

It assists with physical healing. The mind/body connection in healing and the ability of the mind to influence the body are well-known phenomenon. Lucid dreaming has been known to help with healing in general, from warning of health issues to assisting with physical injuries and accessing medical advice.

It solves problems. Whether it's a personal problem or a mathematical one, this state of lucid dreaming can provide you with a suite of answers and you will find a person, ally or spiritual being who can help you. Scientists, inventors and engineers have been able to access this gateway into conscious dreaming and bring back knowledge to their waking world.

It enhances your creativity output. We experience the longest duration of REM sleep just before we wake up. This opens up a huge well of creativity where the dreamer can see things differently and make connections that are outside the norm. Artists, singers, musicians, playwrights, authors, poets and inventors have used their sleep and dreaming time productively, waking up to new ideas and gifting them to the world.

It allows you to share your experience with a friend through dream sharing. More experienced lucid dreamers are able to virtually meet at an allocated place in their dreamscape.

It connects you with your loved ones who have passed. When you become lucid you can have a visitation dreams in which you can communicate with the deceased and hear their messages. Similarly, you will be able to meet your spirit guides, ascended masters, astral beings, allies, totem animals and other spiritual entities.

It can take you through time. If you have full conscious control over a dream you can also use it to travel in time, exploring the future or going back to a past-life experience. Even shared precognitive dreaming is possible. With a little practice you can use lucid dreaming to leave your body and explore the world.

It makes you a consciousness explorer. Lucid dreaming can bring you into contact with the deeper part of yourself, so in times of crisis you can draw on lucidity to help you become more emotionally resilient. It can uplift you and give you spiritual strength in time of challenges, grief and loss.

Beings of light may represent super-conscious figures, vivid and powerful archetypes or those who have died and reside in higher states of consciousness. They can remind you that you have the inner strength and resilience to deal with difficulties or they can show you ways in which you can help others to do the same. You can take it deeper to a more spiritual practice in which you understand that you can become a co-creator of your own reality and understand a larger awareness than the ego. It is more than the mind can imagine alone.

It helps with nightmares. Most people have at least one distressing dream a year and often the nightmare has a recurring theme that is stuck in the memory and replays in full any time any element related to that theme is activated. Lucid dreaming might be helpful by accessing the trauma centre in the brain and allowing you to control the dream.

Once lucid within the nightmare you will become aware that there is no actual danger despite experiencing some fear. You may then be able to break from your habitual response and instead choose how to respond while you are in a conscious dreaming state.

Lucid dreaming is often used in imagery rehearsal therapy (IRT), where a therapist helps you re-imagine a recurring nightmare with a different, more pleasant storyline. You can do this yourself by rescripting the nightmare so it has a more positive outcome.

If you practise creating alternate endings during waking time you will be able to quickly change the script to a positive one while lucid dreaming. In your waking state you might have imagined having a superpower to attack your fear or an ally in the spirit or dream world to assist you in fighting off nightmare fiends. Sometimes, practising putting a white light around you and conjuring a shield of protection are vivid images your mind can store and use in REM when you revisit your nightmare.

A technique to help with excessive fear during a lucid dream nightmare is to take a deep conscious breath, breathing it out and releasing the fear. Another technique is to face tormentors who are threatening you in your nightmares and ask them why they are chasing you and why they want to hurt you. This method will bring about a healing effect and quite often lead to deeper understanding of the nightmare content, allowing for personal transformation.

Many feel that facing fears in dreams helps them with anxiety. I have advised parents whose children have experienced nightmares to get the children to re-imagine the scene of the nightmare and re-script the ending, one in which the child creates their own self-defence system of superpowers and calls on allies to help them face their monster. The sense of control the child feels will help them to overcome day-to-day fears, as the dream confidence will spill over into their waking life. The influence of our imagination on our psyche goes a long way in helping you to soothe and heal.

The power of thought in lucid dreaming can shape and guide our reality. Inner change can affect outer change: when we bring back the inner dream into our outer world it can affect our everyday lives as well as the collective dream of living in a world that is safe and peaceful.

MASTERING LUCID DREAMING

If you really want to harness your creativity like surreal artist Salvador Dali and inventor Thomas Edison you don't need to be asleep to enter the twilight state experienced in the transitional stage from wakefulness to sleep. You know you are in hypnagogia when you experience sensations such as falling, floating, seeing lights, hearing sounds and seeing patterns such as swirls and images. You are ready to enter the sleep state, in which you go no further if you want to expand your creativity and maximise your solution solving or prepare for induced lucid dreaming. Hypnagogia happens at the edges of sleep when you are semi-awake and have enough consciousness to know you are in a particular place such as a room in your home, and is where powerful healing, visions, inspiration and creativity happen.

Both Dali and Edison intentionally stayed awake in the boundary area of creativity that was not a real dreaming state but rather a pre-dreaming state. However, most of us experience one major setback when we are in the borderlands between waking and sleeping: our tiredness. Our heads hit the pillow and all we want to do is sink into a blissful sleep: a rare commodity in an age of frenetic activity and demanding jobs. Some lucid dreamers can't wait to lie down, force their eyelids shut and wait for those colourful swirls and noises to begin so they can induce lucid dreaming. Hypnagogia is not something you can control or force; all you can do is enjoy the sensations it offers but not be lured into sleep. You need to remain totally relaxed but aware.

Dali created a technique he called 'slumber with a key': a brief nap used to channel the hypnagogic state. He recommended the afternoon nap technique to his artist friends to induce a visual inspiration:

> You must seat yourself in a bony armchair, preferably of Spanish style, with your head tilted back and resting on the stretched leather back. Your two hands must hang beyond the arms of the chair, to which your own must be soldered in a supineness of complete relaxation . . .
>
> In this posture, you must hold a heavy key which you will keep suspended, delicately pressed between the extremities of the thumb and forefinger of your left hand. Under the key you will previously have placed a plate upside down on the floor. . . The moment the key drops from your fingers, you may be sure that the noise of its fall on the upside down plate will awaken you.

Just as you fall asleep you experience muscle paralysis that would cause anything you are holding to drop and startle you with the noise of its falling, so you wake up. For Dali it occurred in the short window of time just before awakening when he would enter the hypnagogic sleep state, and was where creative connections of the mind brought together distant ideas and concepts in a new way. This is known as being in your active imagination state, in which you creatively engage with what's in your psyche. You are able to see your internal world of memories and create associations and concepts that have already been explored in your waking mind. This connection between waking ideas and the uninhibited concepts of the mind creates a completely new way of thinking.

Thomas Edison slept for an average of four hours per night but took short, spaced out naps during the day. As with Dali, the nap time occurred in hypnagogia and was when he came up with inventions and solutions to problems. Instead of the key technique, he held steel balls in each hand during his naps that would drop when his grip relaxed. To make sure he would wake up from the sounds of the steel balls, he dropped the balls on a set of metal saucers. With pen and paper close at hand, he would then wake up and note down his ideas. Edison would get comfortable in a chair or work bench rather than a comfortable bed, as the idea was not to sleep but to maximise creative time for productivity and results.

It suited both Dali and Edison to experience the hypnagogic or twilight state as their thinking processes were altered and it resulted in giving them a unique approach to and perspective on their work.

A more natural way our bodies wake up before falling asleep is through myoclonic or hypnic jerks, which occur when the body is preparing to let go and fall asleep. The brain perceives these jerks as potentially falling as we are relinquishing control over our waking bodies.

Being in a hypnagogic state is not always a positive experience, as many lucid dreamers know. Body and brain chemistry changes as it prepares for sleeping and we can wake up but not be able to move, an unpleasant condition known as sleep paralysis (see later in this chapter for more information on sleep paralysis). Our bodies are paralysed so we can't physically act out our dreams, but our brain is conscious. As our brain experiences sights and visions in the hypnagogic state they can become dark and frightening, with the appearance of threatening demons or evil entities.

Although hypnagogia helped Dali and Edison with their creative endeavours, many lucid dreamers induce hypnagogia to take it further into lucid dreaming. This is relatively easy, especially if you are experienced with yoga, mindfulness, meditation or visualisation. It is suitable for a beginning oneironaut but, as with any skill, you need to practise. Try this exercise:

1. Lie down and relax but don't fall asleep.

2. Empty your mind and focus on remaining aware.

3. Gently stare at the back of your eyelids. Look for tiny specks of light and, if they appear, let them go.

4. Allow your eyes to go in and out of focus.

5. As your body enters into a deep relaxed state you may feel waves, then strobes, then eventually dream scenes.

6. Your body will now be at its most relaxed state and you are almost unconscious. Keep fighting the urge to fall asleep. You have entered the state of hypnagogia.

Another twin state of in-between dreaming is called the hypnopompic state (see pages 104, 105, 188), which has more of a drifting sensation and is experienced when you come out of your sleep. Not everyone experiences hypnopompia and you can skip it altogether if the alarm comes on and you suddenly snap out of a dream. A snooze alarm may allow you to re-enter that partial waking state and experience equally powerful experiences and visions. Many visitation dreams from the departed occur during this time, which is another very exciting state to access.

'What is real? If real is what you can feel, smell, taste and see, then "real" is simply electrical signals interpreted by your brain.'

– MORPHEUS, *THE MATRIX*

Before we delve into lucid dreaming techniques it's important to recognise that dreams are in the greater part a reflection of your day-time thoughts. Thinking about your dreams during the day and asking yourself if you are dreaming is a useful practice. Concentrate on how much you want to experience lucid dreaming, and the intent might actualise in your dreams. Seeing cues in your dreams is another way to know you are in a lucid dreaming state. However, in order to learn how to lucid dream there are two important techniques to master: dream recall and reality testing.

DREAM RECALL

There is no practice more effective for inducing lucid dreaming than *dream recall*. Making a consistent effort to remember dreams will help your waking mind connect with your dreaming awareness. This will allow you to become more familiar with your dream content and remember characters, settings, feelings and sensations that may feel unusual in your dream. Your waking reasoning will help you recognise unfamiliar surroundings or dream scenes when you are lucid dreaming.

When you go to bed, instruct yourself to remember your dreams when you wake up in the morning. This setting of intention to remember dreams is an excellent start to increasing dream recall. Popular lucid dream author Charlie Morley suggests in his book, *Lucid Dreaming Made Easy*, that one of the most important steps to lucid dreaming is to set your intention to remember your dream. Before bed and even as you're falling asleep, recite over and over in your mind: 'Tonight I remember my dreams. I have excellent dream recall.' When you wake up, keep your eyes closed and stay still rather than rushing to dive out of bed as soon as the alarm goes off. Remain in bed for a few minutes, and recall as many dream fragments, images and feelings as you can and record them quickly in the dream journal by your bedside. Having a dream journal with a pen close to you is essential.

REALITY TESTING AND REALITY CHECKS

Reality testing (RT) or *reality checks* is a type of mental training you practise during waking. It is a lucid dreaming technique that involves checking your environment several times a day to see whether or not you're dreaming. Scientifically, this method increases metacognition by training your mind to notice your own awareness and is a mental trick that will help you understand whether you are awake or dreaming. If you haven't done lucid dreaming you may wonder why you would need to do reality testing at all, but you use it because a dream only 'feels' like a dream after you've woken up. It seems real enough when you are experiencing the dream, but you can't trust your normal senses to distinguish dream from reality on their own. All waking life rules go out the window when you are in a dream state.

In lucid dreaming, you have to be able to tell the difference between what's real and what's a dream, which is why you need to practise reality testing daily in your waking life. Being mindful during the day is exactly what you do in a lucid dream. Ask yourself: Where am I? What is my goal? What do I want to achieve during my time here? What am I going to do next? How am I feeling?

There are a number of ways to do reality testing and you may choose those that resonate best with you. You can start with one reality check and do it multiple times a day then increase it to two or three times maximum, the idea being that this will train your mind to repeat the reality testing while dreaming, which can then induce lucid dreaming. My personal favourites are fingers through the palm or mirror reality checks (see below). Everyone has a way that works best for them.

I want to stress the importance of reality checks as a gateway into lucid dreaming: don't bypass this practice. The key to reality checks is to genuinely ask yourself if you're dreaming or not and repeat this practice throughout the day so that eventually you start to incorporate it in your dreams. You can set an alarm every two or three hours to remind yourself to do a reality check. Ask yourself: 'Am I dreaming?' Next, check your environment to confirm whether or not you are dreaming. Notice your own awareness and the way in which you are interacting with your surroundings.

Here are common reality checks people use both in their waking life and in their dreams:

- **Breathing:** are you able to pinch your nose and close your mouth shut and still breathe? If you can still breathe you're dreaming.

- **Jumping:** when you jump, do you float back to the ground rather than a have hard landing? If you float you're dreaming.

- **Reading:** can you read the same sentence twice without it changing? Can you read words? Frontal lobe processing and the left/logical hemisphere are muted when dreaming and cannot process the written word. If you can't read a whole sentence or you look away and the words change you're dreaming.

◎ **Vision:** is your vision clearer or blurrier or more magnified than usual? If your vision varies from its normal state you're dreaming.

◎ **Hand position:** can you push your hands through a solid surface? Do they look normal? Are they solid? Look at your hands for a good five to 10 seconds to see if they appear wavy or odd in any way, as they most often do in dreams. Quickly look away and then back at your hand again. In a dream, your brain will usually struggle to reproduce an identical projection of your hand, so on second glance it may look dappled wavy or translucent or have fingers missing. When you look at your hand twice in a row the dreaming brain tries to reproduce exactly the same image but doesn't have the processing speed to do this effectively. If your hands aren't normal you're dreaming.

◎ **Fingers and palm:** take the first two fingers on your right hand and try to press them through the palm of your left hand. If you are dreaming your fingers should move through your palm.

◎ **Reading the time:** can you read a clock face or digital watch? If you're dreaming the time on a clock will constantly change, but if you're awake the time will barely change. Can you find a clock or your watch and read the time? The logical left brain hemisphere recognises and precisely processes numerical sequences via logical filters that are inactive in dreams except to some practised lucid dreamers. Logical filters do not apply to brain function in states of dreaming, hence the wild and weird dream presentations experienced.

- ◎ **Flying:** can you will yourself to fly or hover above the ground? Flying is a classic lucid dream, so if you can make yourself fly you're in a dream state.

- ◎ **Mirror reflection:** does your reflection look normal in a mirror? If you look in the mirror and then look away and back again and your reflection is not normal you're dreaming.

- ◎ **Adding up numbers:** can you add up two numbers correctly? Anything logical in your waking world will be difficult to reproduce in the dreaming world. Numbers and reading, like telling the time, require processing that the dreaming mind can't replicate.

- ◎ **Solid objects:** push your hand against a solid object such as a wall or table and see if it goes through. Practise both in waking life and inside your dream.

Remember to practise these tests daily if you are serious about exploring the world of lucid dreaming. As I mentioned earlier, if you are not a natural lucid dreamer the checks are essential for training your brain to recognise what's real and what's a dream. Once you are inside your dream, check the ones you've selected from your day tests.

WAYS TO ENTER A LUCID DREAM STATE

There are two common ways to enter a lucid dream state:

- ◎ Inside the REM sleep dream in which you are dreaming normally you think to yourself: 'Oh, I'm dreaming.' With the realisation that you are dreaming comes consciousness, and this presence of mind allows you to take control of the dream. This is why it's important to continue the practice of reality checks, as the conscious brain will take over and you will become lucid.

◎ When you are still awake and move into the sleep stage of hypnagogia. If you remain conscious for long enough, then while you are relaxing your body into sleep, hypnagogic visions can take you right into the lucid dream world. You can enter this mind awake/body asleep state through visualisation, meditation, binaural beats and the use of herbal supplements.

I will go back to my initial statement about the idea of controlling your lucid dream: it's not about intending to direct, control or dominate your dream but making friends with the unconscious mind.

> You have to genuinely expect that you can experience being able to fly or breathe underwater or run through walls; you exert your will over the unconscious mind but don't overpower it. Robert Waggoner made this comparison: 'the sailor does not control the ocean.' So, ride the waves of lucid dreaming and listen to what it has to tell you.

TECHNIQUES FOR BETTER LUCID DREAMING

Lucid dreaming is a long-term life skill. You will never stop sleeping and there is no end destination. You will experience dream droughts, as we all do from time to time. You may even want to stop lucid dreaming if you experience recurring and unpleasant side effects such as nightmares and sleep paralysis.

There will always be room to improve and grow with patience and have the mindset that lucid dreaming is a lifelong practice. Being able to connect to your inner core, becoming conscious within the unconscious, provides the possibility of communicating with your own divine potential – your daemon or higher self – and the ability to see how limitless you actually are in the bigger world of expanded consciousness. It's a big deal to be able to glimpse the lucid dreaming world, but don't try to compete with yourself or others with your lucidity prowess.

There are several proven lucid dreaming techniques that will help you to maintain consciousness inside your dream world. You will find more sources in lucid dreaming manuals, online via tutorials or lucid dream conference summits, social media groups, professional dream groups such as the International Association for the Study of Dreams, YouTube videos, radio and TV shows, Ted Talks, blogs, apps and other sources. There is no shortage of information on dreams and lucid dreams.

I briefly cover those basic lucid dreaming techniques I have personally used in my own lucid dreaming journey and those that have been studied by dream research scientists. The information isn't meant to replace a committed effort such as taking lessons and reading books by experienced dream experts and spiritual teachers with a scientific and academic background such as Charlie Morley, Robert Waggoner, Clare Johnson, Patricia Garfield, Deirdre Barrett and Andrew Holecek (refer to the bibliography). Some techniques are less suitable for a regular daily work schedule, however, the more you focus on the various techniques and lucid dreaming in general the more frequently you will have lucid dreams.

Since his breakthrough research into lucid dreaming in 1980s, Dr Stephen LaBerge has become the pioneer of lucid dreaming research. Not only did he construct one of the most popular lucid dreaming techniques, he has also led many scientific studies on the subject. LaBerge's work has helped researchers discover the therapeutic benefits of lucid dreaming, which have been useful in treating conditions such as PTSD, recurring nightmares and anxiety. And to think that previously there was no scientific study to prove that lucid dreaming existed!

MNEMONIC INDUCTION OF LUCID DREAMS

LaBerge created a technique called mnemonic induction of lucid dreams (MILD), one of the first methods to use scientific research to induce lucid dreams. MILD is based on a behaviour called 'prospective memory', which involves setting an intention to do something later. In MILD, you make the intention to remember that you're dreaming. It is an effective technique but a difficult one, as you have to practise it while falling asleep. These are the essential steps:

- ◎ memorise the dream (dream recall)
- ◎ set the intention
- ◎ visualise the lucidity of the dream
- ◎ drop off to sleep or repeat.

Charlie Morley suggested an easy way to remember the order of the MILD technique is to:

- ◎ **M**: memorise the dream you were just having
- ◎ **I**: intention (set the intention)
- ◎ **L**: lucidity (visualise the lucid dream)
- ◎ **D**: drop off to sleep or do it again.

Step 1. Before going to bed use the autosuggestion method below for promoting good dream recall and look over the previous night's dream in your dream journal. When you wake up after any REM period, arouse yourself, recall your dream and learn it off by heart.

Step 2. Get ready to go back to sleep, but before returning to sleep and as you enter the hypnagogic state tell yourself: 'The next time I'm dreaming I want to remember that I'm dreaming.' Say this in your mind with conviction.

Step 3. Visualise you are back in the dream from which you just awoke, remembering it step by step and scene by scene. However, this time see yourself recognising that you're dreaming and become fully lucid. You can imagine yourself doing a reality check or seeing something odd and having the realisation that you're dreaming. Imagine acting out what you might like to do once you're lucid, such as flying.

Step 4. Lie down and focus on your intention and follow this with the visualisation as many times as you can until you drop off to sleep. You may also repeat steps two and three again and allow yourself to fall asleep.

If you are worried about dream recall, know that you already use this form of memory in your daily routines, such as calling someone back or picking up and dropping something off, so you have the ability to carry out intentions for the 'future'. If you are unable to remember a dream when you wake you can still practise MILD; all you need to do is select a recent dreams that you recall well and practise rescripting and rehearsing that dream as if it were lucid.

THE WAKE-BACK-TO-BED TECHNIQUE

If you can't bear to have interrupted sleep the wake-back-to-bed (WBTB) technique may not be the technique for you, even though it is effective for many: you need motivation to follow through. Research has shown that morning naps after a period of wakefulness are very productive times for lucid dreaming because we get more REM or vivid dream sleep activity per sleep cycle as the night progresses. In other words, the more dreams the greater chance of a lucid dream. Also, there is less time between falling asleep and when REM sleep begins than at the start of the night: about 90 minutes compared with five to 20 minutes during a morning nap. We are generally in a better position to sleep more lightly early in the morning.

You may not want to try this during a working week when you need uninterrupted sleep. Weekends and holidays are ideal times to experiment with the technique. Use this method to WBTB:

Go to bed as normal and sleep for around four to six hours (set your alarm clock to wake you up).

◎ Get out of bed and become fully alert. You can drink water, go to the toilet or sit and relax on your bed. Write in your dream journal, read a good book about lucid dreaming or otherwise occupy your mind with something dream related. This period of wakefulness is important for doing something that brings presence of mind.

◎ After about 20 to 30 minutes, go back to bed and relax. You should be in total relaxation, ready to enter a lucid dream state by thinking about dreaming and what you are going to do inside your lucid dream.

◎ Sleep.

The WBTB technique works because it tricks the body into thinking it will be REM deprived. REM sleep is enjoyed by everyone, so be mindful of not waking anyone else if you can avoid it. When given the chance to return to sleep your brain will not hesitate to get back into REM sleep, luxuriating in the bonus REM time that is needed for healthy brain function. The key is to spend the awake time thinking about lucid dreaming. This conscious focus can carry on into the dream world as a reminder that you're dreaming. What's more, when practised over time you'll teach your brain to release its wake up hormones after just six hours of sleep.

AUTOSUGGESTION

A very easily mastered and popular technique to induce lucid dreaming is autosuggestion, which is particularly effective for people used to doing meditation, visualisations or hypnosis. Autosuggestion is about believing you are going to have a lucid dream while you are asleep. As you go to bed or if you awaken during the night, put yourself in the frame of mind of genuinely expecting that tonight or sometime soon you will become conscious within a dream. You can use mantras such as:

> *'I recognise every detail in the dream.'*
> *'Tonight I am connected to my lucid dream.'*
> *'I know I am dreaming.'*

Clearly state to yourself without being pressured the experience of a lucid dream and then let it go. Keep it in the present tense so that your brain will already acknowledge it is going to connect as soon as you begin lucid dreaming. Try to genuinely expect to have a lucid dream; it may sound too simple, but it does work.

WAKE-INITIATED LUCID DREAMING

Like autosuggestion, wake-initiated lucid dreaming (WILD) is another effective and popular way to experience lucid dreaming. This mind awake/body asleep technique will help you reach and enter a lucid dream from your waking state:

- Lie down on your bed with your eyes closed. You can also do this after waking during the night.

- Relax, focusing on your breath and simply observing any thoughts that arise without getting caught by them. If you do, snap back and focus again on your breath. Meditate if you can.

- Concentrate on the darkness behind your closed eyes. As you enter the hypnagogic state, gently focus your awareness on any images, sounds or sensations, simply letting it all float by you.

- Begin to visualise with as much close-up detail as possible to increase your visual awareness. The trick is not to engage in the scenes until the dreamscape is formed in a solid way so that you drop into it consciously. You will be building layers in your mind until your landscape solidifies.

- Your body should be already asleep while your mind should be still awake, and as the dream imagery pulls you forward you're into your lucid dream.

USING CANDLES

A good visual practice to help enter the lucid dream state is the candle technique, which I use to prepare for lucid dreaming:

- Light a candle and watch the candlelight.

- Close your eyes and imagine it in your mind's eye.

- Practise increasing the dream image daily; it will become habit that when you close your eyes to go to sleep you will see the candlelight.

- When you see the candle in your dream you will know you're lucid dreaming.

SENSES-INITIATED LUCID DREAMING

Senses-initiated lucid dreaming (SSILD) is a fairly new technique for which data is now emerging. SSILD is a hybrid lucid dreaming technique that combines aspects of multiple techniques such as the ones described above. Like WBTB, it involves waking up after five hours of sleep and then repeatedly focusing your attention on visual, auditory and physical sensations for 20 seconds each before returning to sleep. The core component of SSILD is following a cycle in which you focus on the three senses of sight, hearing and touch in a consistent manner. It's similar to mindfulness meditation but more involved, repeatedly shifting your focus.

The key findings of the International Lucid Dream Induction Study (ILDIS) by Denholm Aspy at the University of Adelaide, published in mid-2020, showed that the MILD technique was the most effective for inducing lucid dreams. Equally, the SSILD technique also proved to be very successful even for those who had never had a lucid dream before. Interestingly, people who did MILD by itself had slightly more lucid dreams than people who did both MILD and reality testing. Reality testing on its own did not score too well as an effective lucid dreaming induction technique, at least for short periods such as one week; however, reality testing was an essential element of lucid dreaming. It is best to use reality testing as a supplementary technique rather than a primary one.

WHAT ELSE CAN HELP WITH LUCID DREAMING?

Why are brain waves important in sleep and dreams? Your brain is always creating electrical impulses that travel in the form of brain waves; the faster the waves travel the more awake and alert you are. The most alert form of waves are beta waves. When you are in beta state you're awake, alert and moving. As you slow down and become more relaxed you move into alpha waves. If you're asleep you're having either theta or delta waves. Delta waves are very slow and occur when you are in the deepest state of sleep and relaxation.

As you sleep through the night your brain cycles through alpha, theta and delta waves. When you dream your brain waves move into the theta state, where your mind is alert but you're not physically or consciously aware of it. If you are woken up during this state you'll remember your dream; however, if you wake up during alpha waves you'll be alert and refreshed but not likely to remember your dreams. The ideal time to experience lucid dreaming is in between alpha and theta states: you're not too asleep but not too awake either.

How can you artificially induce this brain-wave state? Exposure to sound waves, known as binaural beats, has been proven to be very helpful for inducing lucid dreaming as well as providing other benefits such as deep sleep, relaxation and reducing insomnia and anxiety.

Binaural beats occur when the sine waves within a close range from the rhythms, sounds or music you hear while sleeping are presented to each ear separately. When you are exposed to two different frequencies at the same time, one in each ear, your brain perceives a *single* tone that is the difference between the two separate frequencies and tunes into the new frequency. If you hear 400Hz in your left ear and 410Hz in your right ear your brain will actually make up the 10Hz in the left ear. The 10Hz your brain makes up is the binaural beat. By altering the frequencies you can actually control the beats your brain creates.

Research indicates that listening to the sounds that create a low-frequency tone triggers a slow down in brain-wave activity – which may help you relax and make it easier to fall asleep and lucid dream. Music is the food for the soul, and I highly recommend listening to binaural beats during hypnagogia.

HERBAL SUPPORT

Only about 20 to 30 per cent of the population are natural lucid dreamers, but there are supplements you can add to your regimen that may help boost your ability to lucid dream. *I would not recommend using any of these unless you first have a health check done by your doctor.* Herbs such as star anise, nutmeg, rosemary and mugwort can be made into a tea and are great for boosting memory. Vitamin B6 (pyridoxine) can improve detailed dream recall and is also good for memory.

Some of the most popular herbal supplements in the lucid dreaming community include melatonin, a natural sleep aid that can also enhance REM sleep and, as a result, increase your chances of lucid dreaming. Bitter grass or dream herb (*Calea zacatechichi*), passionflower, sun opener and blue lotus flower are more exotic hallucinogens but they are not ideal for everyone. Be aware of the side effects and potentially dangerous interactions with prescription or other natural medication. Galantamine is an enzyme inhibitor used for the treatment of Alzheimer's disease and it's becoming well known for its effectiveness in inducing lucid dreaming. However, galantamine is only in the initial stages of testing and can have serious side effects, so I would not recommend taking this without medical advice.

Rather than relying on the crutch of supplements, the best way to lucid dream is to follow the techniques and practices listed above and to establish a good sleep pattern and eat well. Limit caffeine and alcohol intake before bed and do some form of exercise daily. You can eat yourself lucid by ingesting trytophan-rich foods such as chicken, turkey, beans and hard cheeses before bed, unless you have dietary requirements or health issues. Having plenty of magnesium and including calcium-rich foods such as sardines, white bait, almonds, sesame seeds and hard cheeses in your diet will also make a difference. Eating early is best for your dream practice as it is easier for the body to be rested after your food has been digested. All the attention then goes to the brain, which is fired up for dreaming.

SUMMARY OF TIPS FOR LUCID DREAMING

In a nutshell, the following are the best tips to induce lucid dreaming.

Invent dream activities. When you have your first lucid dream the thrill of it can wake you up, especially if you're not sure what to do next (see the next section about dream collapse). To continue past those first few moments of lucidity, plan in advance something specific to do in your next lucid dream. Let your imagination take you anywhere.

Make reality testing a habit. Always test first and then decide whether or not you are dreaming. Also, throughout the day ask yourself as often as you can remember whether you are dreaming, and perform a test to find out. This will carry over by habit to the dream state.

Be patient and persistent. You can't learn to be proficient in a sport or play a musical instrument in just a few weeks. Although many people experience success in lucid dreaming the first night or during the first couple of weeks, it is a skill that requires time and focus to master. Don't try too hard; be relaxed and playful, and allow the dreaming to happen in its own time. Practise over a few months and find a friend to share with.

Don't overdo it. Some new lucid dreamers become obsessed with being as lucid as possible as fast as possible, an approach that doesn't work in the long run. Lucid dream experiences are powerful and often have profound, long-lasting emotional effects in your waking world. Maintain balance and be grounded as you journey into the lucid world of dreams. Sleep well, remain socially connected, walk and exercise and concentrate on practical daily tasks to help you remain focused on reality.

Have expectation and intent. These are key elements to successful lucid dreaming. If you fully expect to create your dreamscape and sequence and you set the intent to be able to do extraordinary things or simply receive a creative gift it will happen. It's really about not being half-hearted but embracing the full possibilities of your imaginative powers.

WHAT CAN GO WRONG

Lucid dreaming is not always a fantastical experience with rainbows, fairy dust and unicorns. There can be negative aspects to lucid dreaming, and it's important you are aware of the side effects of induction techniques:

- ◎ *Sleep problems*: WBTB and MILD involve waking up in the middle of the night, interruptions that can make it difficult to get enough rest especially if you have a sleep disorder or an irregular sleep schedule.

- ◎ *Dream collapses*: for beginners, it's disappointing not to be able to hold on to a dream. See the section below.

- ◎ *False awakenings*: this is what happens when you're in the middle of an activity and think you've woken up but then realise you're still dreaming. See the section below.

- ◎ *Depression*: the sleep interruptions of induction techniques may increase depressive symptoms, especially if you suffer from sleep problems such as insomnia.

- ◎ *Sleep paralysis*: lucid dreaming may occur with sleep paralysis, which can be brief yet terrifying. Lucid nightmares are also another potential negative side effect (see more below).

When dealing with any mind practice, make sure you follow guidelines from experts and reputable practitioners. You can also join lucid dreaming online groups to share your experiences.

Lucid dreaming is *not* dangerous; it's a natural phenomenon that has existed in all cultures since early civilisation. The ancient Egyptians wrote about dreams and the fact they were aware while dreaming, and Tibetan Buddhists have been using dream yoga (a form of lucid dreaming) for thousands of years. Many are born with a natural ability to lucid dream, and have been doing so all of their lives.

LUCID DREAM COLLAPSE

You can become so excited to finally achieve lucid dreaming that you wake up after just getting into it. The first time this happened for me was when I was dreaming about jumping on the back of a lion and riding it like at a rodeo. The sheer exhilaration of being able to do that snapped me out of the dream after a few seconds.

To avoid the dream fading or collapsing, next time you are in a lucid dream and to avoid having it fade or collapse, stay calm and pretend all is normal then rub your hands together. This action will stimulate the conscious mind and keep you focused on your dream body. Next, do a reality test by looking at your hands and asking yourself: 'Am I dreaming?' Finally, if nothing has worked so far, say 'clarity now' in your mind, demanding that your lucid mind provide you with a more vivid dreamscape.

Robert Waggoner suggests that when we experience fear in a lucid dream it will collapse, due partly to the dream asking us to do something outside our comfort zone. Our deeper self or larger awareness is asking us to do this, but we're not ready or unwilling. So, we shut down and the dream collapses. If you're going to go deep to face your shadow and integrate with it you must face your fear.

FALSE AWAKENINGS

Have you ever woken up in your bed, taken a shower, started to eat breakfast or stack the dishwasher only to then wake up for real and realise that you were dreaming? That's a false awakening. Sometimes things are surreal and it's very obvious that you're in a dream, while at other times things appear to be so normal you can't figure out whether you're really awake or not. It can happen more than once in a dream. In a false awakening loop you wake from your dream only to find you're still in a dream, then you wake up again but you're still in the dream, and so the cycle continues. It's annoying, disturbing, uncomfortable and a little frightening to feel trapped within your dream without being able to wake up.

To figure out whether you're awake or experiencing a false awakening, carry out a series of reality checks. Doing reality checks daily will increase your levels of awareness, which will also be enhanced by adding a mindfulness practice. Once you realise you're dreaming you can turn your false awakening into a lucid dream.

LUCID NIGHTMARES

Even though lucid dreams are more vivid and memorable, I don't believe they make nightmares worse or more frequent.

It's important to point out the difference between an ordinary nightmare and a lucid nightmare. If you experience an ordinary nightmare in which you become lucid it is not a lucid nightmare. A lucid nightmare is a bad dream with full conscious awareness from the onset. Just because you are aware of your surroundings does not mean you can control or predict everything in a dream. When you lucid dream your unconscious mind can decide to focus on something scary, which will end up as a lucid nightmare. You may sometimes feel trapped in the nightmare, are unable to wake up or experience a false awakening. Some of the characteristics of lucid nightmares include physical pain, lack of dream control and confrontations with powerful forces. Fortunately, lucid nightmares are not very common.

As with regular dreams and nightmares, scary lucid dreams are reflections of your subconscious mind in which your brain processes negative and sad emotions from your waking life. You may be suppressing traumas or old fears that act out in your dreams. The emotions induced from watching violent or scary movies or playing violent games may carry over into your dreams. Other than a good sleep routine, teach yourself to remain calm in the dream or nightmare. Controlling your nightmare while you are in a lucid dream – such as changing the dream ending, refusing to be the victim or facing your terror – can actually help you overcome nightmares and general fears from your waking life.

Lucid nightmares present a unique opportunity to learn more about yourself: in facing your fears you will be empowering yourself.

SLEEP PARALYSIS

Sleep paralysis is the feeling of being conscious but unable to move or speak. You are still in a partial dream state when you awake into the paralysis, not enough to be alert but enough that you are aware of not being able to move. It is terrifying and feels like a real paralysis, and can last for a few seconds up to a few minutes although it often feels much longer. This state of relaxation is called *atonia*; it is when electrical impulses are cut off from the brain to the muscles, which prevents us from moving and acting out our dreams.

Although sleep paralysis can be scary, it is common and is actually a protective mechanism to prevent you from physically acting out your dreams. During REM sleep you have vivid dreams while your muscles are in REM atonia. However, during sleep paralysis you wake up *before* the REM cycle and REM atonia are finished. You will be conscious, but your body's ability to move hasn't been turned back on yet as the muscles haven't received the signal from the brain to switch on. Basically, you've woken up before you've stopped dreaming. Sleepwalking occurs when the muscles turn on *before* the dreaming is finished and the sleepwalker acts out their dream.

Sleep paralysis can occur when you are falling asleep (hypnagogia) or when you are waking up (hypnopompia), the liminal states of borderline sleep. This state of being consciously awake when your body's asleep is unlike sleep terrors and nightmares. Night terrors are episodes of screaming or intense fear that happen while still asleep and often include sleepwalking, especially in children. When you have a nightmare you are acting inside the dream, that is, the scene takes place inside the dream state (usually REM if it's a vivid dream).

I have experienced bouts of sleep paralysis and it took a huge mental effort to shake myself fully awake from the fear of whatever dream I was experiencing. The unpleasant aspect of sleep paralysis is that it is commonly accompanied by a sensation of being held down by an evil presence or entity that stops you from being able to move. It can be a terrifying experience if you don't understand what's happening. When you are in this partial dream-like state your fears instantly surface. It's a rational response for the mind to create an evil entity that seems to be holding you down, although according to dream expert Anthony Peake the experience is nothing more than a manifestation of the panic brought on by sleep paralysis. The combination of atonia and waking up before the REM stage is over transfers strong dream material into your awakened state while you still can't move.

As if the frozen state isn't bad enough, the common features of sleep paralysis include lying in bed paralysed and hearing strange noises, voices, a frightening presence in the room, creatures, feelings of being held down (such as a demon sitting on your chest), difficulty breathing, being touched and the presence of aliens. You may not only feel an evil presence but may also think that someone or something is touching you or have a sense of breathlessness.

The sleep paralysis phenomenon has been documented since ancient times and from all cultures. The evil entity varies in each tradition, but essentially sleep paralysis was thought to be a demon, witch, hag, ghost, evil genie or alien attacking the dreamer. Usually the method used was sucking the breath out of the dreamer or attempting to smother them while pressing hard on their chest. In the modern era, we understand the mechanics of dream sleep paralysis as being in a mixed state between sleep and wakefulness, the result of our mind manifesting our fears via our imagination. Some dreamers have even felt as though they were sexually abused during the sleep paralysis episode.

At a more collective level the old hag egregore is still being reported. An *egregore* is a concept that represents a thought form, personality or group mind that develops among groups and influences their thoughts. Additionally, the archetypes of incubi and succubi in sleep paralysis are common. What is even more mysterious is the modern evil entity known as the *hat man:* a concept so popular it has its own social media group. Some experts believe the idea of the hat man came from subconsciously merging a composite of scary figures from pop culture such as Freddy Krueger and Michael Myers, which have influenced entire generations. The shape of the terrifying hat man varies, but dreamers all share the same emotions of being paralysed with terror and feeling breathless as fear has sucked the life out of them.

Paralysis is commonly experienced by lucid dreamers who, like regular dreamers, can experience meeting with the old hag, shadow people, demons, goblins and manifestations of their fears. Those who want to induce sleep paralysis to enter the lucid dreaming state, for example, and engage in sleep-paralysis induction will usually end up in this scary state. It may be they feel as though they are dead but in a false awakening lucid dream where the mind is awake but the body is still asleep.

Those who practise out-of-body experiences can be frightened into moving out of or separating from their bodies. The danger experienced in sleep paralysis while lucid dreaming is that the dream can become locked with false awakening loops, the eternal nightmare where fears continue to be manifested. Some successfully practise wake-induced lucid dreaming and are able to astral project out of it.

Between 8 and 50 per cent of people experience sleep paralysis regardless of age and gender, but the frequency is higher in people under the age of 25 years. We know that a lack of sleep and/or stress are contributing factors to sleep paralysis, which will also occur more regularly if you sleep on your back.

Try the following tips to overcome sleep paralysis.

Control your fear and remain relaxed. This can be very difficult to do because your brain is convinced that the images and sensations you see during the phase are real and not hallucinations. Repeat statements in your head such as 'It's only a dream', 'I am safe', 'I am having a sleep paralysis' or 'I can go anywhere', or remain as rational as you can and try to understand the situation without the fear blocking you.

To relax your body, focus on your breath and breathe slowly and deeply as you would for meditation. This may be tricky if you see an evil entity on your lungs and you find it hard to breathe, but ignore the image and focus on your breathing.

Move. Any movement you make will help you wake up and release you from the paralysis, but it takes a major effort to do so. I recall my own sleep paralysis when I tried to move my finger to lift my dream pillow off my face and make a sound. It was a huge effort for me, but if you do this it will activate your brain, which will send a signal to your body to wake up.

Induce sleep paralysis in a lucid dream. It sounds counterintuitive to want to create a frightening experience, but it can be used as a door to lucid dreaming and out-of-body experiences. By being lucid or in a conscious dream state you can control the scene. For example, you can see yourself in your favourite place – a garden, beach, forest, shopping centre – and imagine as many details as you can, including whether you are alone, the time of day, weather, sounds, taste, texture and so on. Keep focusing on positive thoughts and sensations. Although lucid dreaming doesn't cause sleep paralysis, methods such as WILD will increase the frequency of it.

One dreamer shared with me her experience of sleep paralysis and how she eventually overcame it. I was interested in how she knew she was going to have the paralysis before it actually began:

> I felt as if I was being attacked by evil spirits or entities because the paralysis would start with a ringing in my ears. I was absolutely terrified as I thought I was going to be attacked in my sleep and fought the entities off the best way I could and at the same time try to wake myself up. Eventually, I learned to remain calm through these episodes by telling myself that I was not afraid and that I could outsmart them. I remembered to keep breathing and concentrate on my breath. This shifted my focus and the fear finally went away. Eventually I stopped having sleep paralysis.

Psychic attacks in out-of-body experiences can come during the witching hours of 2 am and 4 am, when they say the veil is thinnest between dimensions, worlds and astral planes. Another dreamer reported her experience: 'When the attack comes it usually starts with the covers being pulled off me. The covers are usually on my face and body and I feel that I am about to suffocate. But the fear of the covers being pulled off me is greater. I just know that I have to grab the covers before they begin to slide off. It's terrifying.'

OUT-OF-BODY EXPERIENCES OR ASTRAL PROJECTIONS

Imagine your body floating away from you but you are completely aware of it. Astral projection is an out-of-body experience (OBE) where the astral or soul body separates from the physical body and allows you to go anywhere in the universe you wish to and meet up with other consciousnesses travelling on the astral plane, including people you know.

Everyone has the ability to enter the astral plane. It can occur naturally for some people, but for others it's induced and therefore needs practise and patience to master. As OBE author Robert Monroe claimed: 'We are more than our physical bodies.'

Lucid dreaming happens when you are asleep, taking place within your personal mind-vision experience. With OBEs you experience the sensation of coming out of your physical body so, for example, you can see yourself lying on the bed. Your self-awareness is in a different place to the physical body, and that projection of your mind makes you realise you are more than your physical body. You move beyond physical boundaries in an OBE experience. Your environment and body may not be in your own consciousness but tapping into a wider awareness, expanding beyond the restrictions of your psyche. Ancient mystics and shamans familiar with the astral planes were clear that the physical dimension in which you live is not the only one that exists (see Chapter 7 for further information). It is generally thought there are another six dimensions our soul selves can visit and manifest on, so our soul body is capable of multidimensional presence.

How long you can be out of the physical body will depend on the amount of life force the soul or 'consciousness' has during the process of astral departure or separation for the sleeping host. Similar to lucid dreaming, people may experience sleep paralysis during an OBE. There are beneficial ways to use the paralysis state while astral projecting, such as tuning in to kundalini (life force) energy and going into a meditative state. When we have an awakening experience the kundalini energy spirals upward from its coiled position at the base of the spine, activating each chakra with its energy flowing through us.

It obviously takes practice to master astral projection. A beginner will instantly want to jump back into their body, which will also pull them out of their dream. Once you can journey outside of your physical body you may be free to visit people and places on the physical plane as well as other dimensions of reality.

> In the astral plane your dream body (light body or avatar) is your natural body; it can assume the shape of your thoughts and desires. You may have had OBEs during your night dreams but not recognised them. Do you dream of flying or falling, or wake up with a jolt as though something has dropped inside your body? Or do you have dreams within dreams (false awakenings)? These experiences may well have been journeys outside the body.

Inducing OBEs is similar to the techniques used in lucid dreaming; many practitioners use the MILD technique with the following elements, which for a beginner would be from a wake-induced state into an OBE.

Relaxation. You need to be in protected space with no interruptions. Relax your mind and focus on your breathing. Meditate if you are able to. Remember you need to be in good health to astral project as it takes a lot of energy to be out of your physical body.

Lift off. There are several ways to astral project. One way is to imagine pulling on and climbing a rope with your inner body tugged out of your physical body as continue to climb further up the rope. As you climb higher you will feel yourself start to vibrate, but the whole time you need to relax and concentrate. You may be able to use special breathing techniques or use other stimuli to change your energy field so you can leave your body in a similar way. You can do this with an object that you imagine reaching out and hold onto, using it to pull yourself free of your body. I have spoken to a number of OBE students who find the physical strain of trying to pull out of their body a stumbling block. It does take mental strain to imagine a physical extraction.

One method that has been successful is the movement method, where you imagine something is moving you either in a swaying motion or some other type of motion that you can easily get used to the feel of. This method is very powerful and can almost throw you out of your body if it is directed correctly. Trampolining is another good one: imagine yourself jumping and with every bounce see yourself going a bit higher until your consciousness moves further away from your body and begins to separate.

Have no fear. This is the most difficult part of the process, as it takes a great deal of work to have the confidence to leave your body. If you are fearful you are likely to experience sleep paralysis, hence why it's important to remain calm and relaxed and overcome the barrier of fear. While in projection the astral body and the physical body are linked by an energy flow known as the 'silver cord'. Some people have concerns that the astral body and the dream body can become permanently split if the silver cord is cut. For those experiencing a near-death experience (NDE) the silver cord becomes severed only when approaching physical death.

One dreamer explained the cord connection as being an umbilical cord:

> I floated across the floor staring at my body sleeping motionless in bed . . . My umbilical cord was attached to my belly button and stretching back to my physical body in bed. Although I felt calm, I was puzzled why the umbilical cord was there . . . On my return I noticed my umbilical cord still attached to me until I was safely back in bed.

Imagine your body spinning. When you reach the sleep paralysis or vibration stage you should vividly imagine your astral body spinning around vigorously and try to make it feel as real as possible. If you imagine this spinning motion correctly you should start to feel dizzy and disorientated, and all you have to do is imagine yourself rolling out of your body and you will be out!

Focus on the intention. While lying down, focus your mind on the intention to have an OBE. Keep repeating the purpose silently in your mind, for example, 'I now experience astral projection'. Once you find yourself in the humming and vibrations stage of lift off go OBE with an intent you created in your waking state: think about, for instance, whether you could return to your childhood home and picture yourself there. If you are after some healing, consider creating a ball of light to place on your body where it needs it most. The important thing is that you need clarity of purpose. Formulate your intent in your waking state and execute the plan when in the OBE.

Select a physical object around you. This may be a door or window in your room. Try to imagine yourself walking, floating, gliding or bouncing around your home.

The candle method. The candle method is a way of concentrating on an object such as a candle to stay focused on the point right as you enter an OBE. You'll be able to stare at the flame for longer, which means you'll find it easier to have an OBE. It works because all the time you're staring at the candle flame you're maintaining your focus on one thing, which is key for astral projection and will help you easily slip outside of your body. People also say that focusing on the flame relaxes you so much due to the mesmerising ambience that it just makes the whole thing easier.

Focusing on the flame will also leave an after image on your inner eyelids so that when you close your eyes, and if you do it right, you'll already have a dot you can see while your eyes are closed and you can more easily focus on your third eye chakra energy and astral project that way. I have found this to be a useful exercise when I want to put myself in a trance-like state in order to reflect deeply, be creative and get in touch with my deeper inner self.

Projection. Sometimes an OBE can happen spontaneously, but it's more likely that the majority have to intentionally try to project themselves. When you leave your body move away from it. This will prevent you from being immediately snapped back in. Explore and familiarise yourself with your surroundings. Notice the vibrations as they increase to allow yourself to explore the many dimensions.

You may be rising above your house and into the moonlit sky and continue your journey up all the way into space, maybe even hovering above the blue haze of the ionosphere of planet Earth. You decide after dancing among the twinkling stars to descend back to your house and enter your bedroom through an open window, where you notice your sleeping body. At this point you can slide back into your bed and inside your body. What a trip of a lifetime!

Return. A common question is: how long does projection last? How long you can be out of your physical body will depend on the amount of life force your soul or consciousness has during the process of astral departure or separation from your body. It can range from a few seconds to a couple of hours. To re-enter your body imagine being pulled back inside or slipping back into your physical skin, like you were putting on an item of clothing.

Record your experiences. After each astral projection, keep a record of your experiences. It's important to keep a journal to record all of your dreams and astral projections as they serve to give you insight into your psyche and help you to navigate the astral world more confidently as you become more familiar with the landscape. Try to note the amount of time you spent outside of your physical body.

DREAM YOGA

Lucid dreaming and dream yoga have been practised as a means of attaining spiritual transcendence by wisdom traditions such as the Toltecs, Tantrics, Sufis, Gnostic Christians, shamans, indigenous peoples and especially Tibetan Buddhists. Dream yoga author and spiritual teacher Andrew Holecek describes the difference between dream yoga and lucid dreams as: 'Dream yoga starts where lucid dreaming leaves off. While lucid dreaming is mostly psychological in nature and concerned with self-fulfilment, dream yoga is spiritual in nature and concerned with self-transcendence. It is not concerned with dream content, but with how you relate to and then transform that content.'

In lucid dreams we work on our psychological issues, facing grief and unresolved problems and even predicting our future. Dream yoga transcends but includes lucid dreaming, so lucid dreaming has to be part of the dream yoga practice. In dream yoga lucid dreams are a laboratory that is used to look deeply into the nature of the mind. Author and world-renowned teacher of dream yoga Charlie Morley explains that a lucid dream is where the conscious mind gets not only to explore but also to use the unconscious mind. Given that some neuroscientists suggest that as much as 95 per cent of our brain activity is unconscious, a whole new world opens up.

The world is made up of the nature of mind. LaBerge states: 'When we dream, waking consciousness is dreaming consciousness without sensory constraints.' What we can do in the waking world we can do in dreams; as above in dream worlds, so too below in the physical world. In other words, dream yoga shows how lucid dreaming leads to lucid living. Waking up and becoming lucid in our dreams demonstrates how we can wake up and become more lucid (aware) in daily life. This is the 'yoga' part, which shows us how to stretch lucidity into all states.

The main difference between lucid dreaming and dream yoga is that the latter is a way to prepare for death. Morley says: 'In Buddhism, dream yoga is an opportunity to explore emptiness, and to explore beyond the mind.' It allows the person to wake up in dreaming and prepare for realms beyond death. According to Tibetan Buddhism, the mental body we have after death is almost identical to the mental body we have in dreams, and the experiences in dreams and death are also similar.

By bringing the light of lucidity into the darkness of ignorance – sleep – with dream and sleep yoga we not only illuminate and eventually eliminate non-lucid sleep and dreaming but also non-lucid death. When brought to fruition, not only does lucid dreaming lead to lucid living, it also leads to lucid dying.

The techniques of dream yoga are similar to lucid dreaming techniques, with added spiritual elements and practices such as meditation. The throat chakra is the dream or expression chakra in Tibetan Buddhism, the soul expressing itself both in waking life and in dreams. Directing energy to this area as you are falling asleep or just before will help with lucidity.

The progression to sleep and dream yoga goes like this: first you learn how to remember your dreams; then you learn how to wake up in them; then you train your mind in the dream; then you learn how to stay awake in dreamless sleep. All the while you are taking the insights from the night and transferring them into the day. Not only are you transforming the night into meditation, but you begin to transform your life. You start to wake up in the spiritual sense. Result: an enlightened and awakened life.

THE BARDO STATE

When we die we transition from one state to the next. Tibetan Buddhism holds that experiencing a lucid dream at our death is known as being in a *bardo* state, or the transitional state between birth and rebirth. Each night when we lie down to sleep we are actually rehearsing for death – we are motionless, our eyes are closed – except that our bodies are alive. Common idioms reinforce this view of deep, restful sleep as being a kind of death: 'sleep like the dead' and 'dead to the world'.

How many times have you shaken your sleeping child or partner as they lay there motionless in deep sleep, waiting for a slight movement to reassure you they were alive? We humans are wired to be super vigilant when it comes to survival.

Lucid dream training is used to prepare for the after-death bardo state, the dream-like hallucinatory experience you enter into once your mind stream has separated from your body at the point of death. If you can truly master lucid dreaming then at the point of death you can become lucid within the dream-like, after-death bardo, recognise the nature of mind and reach full spiritual enlightenment. As you fall asleep you enter a watered-down version of when you die: you fall into deep, dreamless (deathless) sleep. A difficult after-death journey is a non-lucid journey. If you don't have a lucid dream and wake up and take control in the bardo state, what takes over? According to Anthony Holecek, your habits are actually lower vibrations in which you put self-awareness into a state of auto pilot.

Along with lucid dreaming, the ancient practice of dream yoga is used as a preparation for death, dying and the after-death state. Tibetan Buddhists believe the fear of death can be removed, that we can control the after-death journey with a lucid dreaming mind. Westerners don't deal with death very well – it's not often talked about – but we can alleviate anxiety about dying through altered state practices. We can meet our moment of death with joy and acceptance, as in the moment of our death we can be at peace. For Tibetan Buddhists, death is a life released from sensory constraints and an opportunity for growth as part of our evolution.

As profound as dream yoga is, there is actually a further step. With some skill in lucid dreaming and dream yoga you can progress into sleep yoga, which is where you maintain lucidity or awareness even during deep dreamless sleep.

BECOMING AN AWAKENED DREAMER

During the time I was writing this chapter on lucid dreaming I was able to overcome my own sleep paralysis nightmare. I did a lot of research and intensive writing during the day and before bedtime, so it's not surprising the words acted as autosuggestion and my dream recall was triggered on high alert mode. In my lucid dream I found myself in sleep paralysis, with a threatening entity pushing on my chest and trying to frighten me and extinguish my breath. I remembered the lucid dream research and kept calm, and more importantly knew that I could breathe and breathed slowly. I recall smiling to myself and feeling quietly confident.

But that was only part one of the sleep paralysis: the dark shadowy figure was incensed that I should win so easily and made itself bigger, its shadow engulfing my bedroom as it swooped down to attack me. I felt momentarily stunned as it placed its enormous gaping mouth on mine as if to eat me then totally engulfed me in its body, all the time attempting to suck the breath out of me. Once again I felt a sense of calm and breathed into the situation in measured, steady breaths. I felt perfectly fine and willed myself to wake up not because I was afraid, but to congratulate myself on achieving this great feat that for years had eluded me. I woke up victorious, wrote my experience down right away in my dream journal, had a warm beverage and went back to bed.

It was during the witching hour of 3.15 am that I had woken up, and within an hour I was asleep and slept a blissful sleep with a smug grin on my face. I had won the battle. I felt this sense of victory for days after, and in bringing this emotion to my waking world I was able to handle stresses that normally would have overwhelmed me. I could help people who needed comfort and advice during this time without me feeling drained. The dream had given me energy.

And that is one of the gifts of lucid dreaming. Like in the Hero's journey, the hero brings back the elixir to his ordinary world and then uses it to help others.

THE WITCHING HOUR

If you are awake at 3.00 am you'll find it is a powerful time that has long been considered special. It is known by the terms the *witching hour*, the devil's hour, angel o'clock, the hour of God, the hour of the wolf and the hour of the muse, and it has traditionally been thought to be a time when there are high levels of energy and spirit activity.

In the Chinese meridian system 3.00 am to 5.00 am is when the lung meridian (an energy stream in the body related to the lungs) is most active. The lungs represent the breath of life and hold the energetic emotion of grief, so waking between these hours with a sense of breathlessness, stolen breath, holding your breath or breathing difficulties is an ancient symbolism of death and grief via the taking of the breath of life.

The witching hour came about as a reference to wizards and witches who slept a few hours in the day and a few hours in the night, rising with the sun and the moon. They watched over the night, held the space of light in the dark and oversaw people's souls until around 3.00 am, when they would sleep for another two to four hours and were therefore not being guardians of light for the people when they rested and slept in those night hours. These were known as the witching hours or haunting times in the dark of the night and were believed to be the most common times for the devil to be active.

Other significant incidents that take place during these hours include melatonin levels peaking in the pineal gland, peaks in the earth's heartbeat (Schumann's resonance), most clouds forming, the majority of heart failures and deaths, the most creative time for inspiration and creating ideas and many near-death experiences occur. It is the time when sleep is the deepest but nightmares are the most real. If you have insomnia it is the time when you can be haunted by your deepest fears.

As we age we begin to suffer from sleep fragmentation, which means we wake up in the middle of the night and find it difficult to fall back to sleep. It is a predatory insomnia when we lie awake feeling vulnerable, hopeless and worried about everything, including not getting enough sleep. Conversely, the hour of God (between

2 am and 4 am) is when you wake up at this same time and feel calm, and there is no artificial light to disrupt your circadian rhythm. The mystic Sufi poet Rumi advised those who could not fall asleep to remain awake because the universe has secrets to share:

The breezes at dawn have secrets to tell you.
Don't go back to sleep!
You must ask for what you really want.
Don't go back to sleep!
People are going back and forth across the doorsill where the two worlds touch.
The door is round and open.
Don't go back to sleep.

Rumi's poem reminds us that, as lucid dreamers, being awake prepares us for the next awakened dream journey.

FROM
DREAM
TIME TO
REAL TIME.

Chapter 7

SHAMANIC DREAMING

'We are Earth people on a journey to the stars. Our quest, our Earth walk is to look within, to know who we really are, to see that we are connected to all things, that there is no separation, only in the mind.'

– SPIRITUAL WARRIOR LAKOTA SEER

'Sometimes dreams are wiser than waking.'

– BLACK ELK OF THE OGLALA LAKOTA PEOPLE

In times of great change many people turn within and follow spiritual practices that are firmly grounded in the natural world. At such times our personal losses at a micro level serve to propel us into the collective grieving of the planet, while at a global level we may suffer through natural disasters that threaten our very existence.

> Shamans believe we can dream a new world into being, that we are co-creators of our universe but that first we need to heal ourselves.

Many are drawn to shamanic principles and practices because of its relevance today and as we find ourselves in conflict with our environment. This chapter focuses on the dreaming aspect of the shamanic path, especially in relation to healing and creating a positive future for our community, the planet and ourselves. We are a single species, and what we have in common is our humanity. We need to take the time to reflect on what really matters.

Everyone can dream but not everyone becomes a dreamer. To be a dreamer is a long-term practice and passion for a greater depth of understanding of the interior life, of connection to nature and the collective global community. How do we remember our dreams? By sharing them, of course. In indigenous communities dream recall is valued and is a part of everyday life. Asking a person 'What did you dream last night?' is a regular morning ritual, and the dreams are shared with family members and the community. Naturally, this means dream recall is high, and dream recollection is a natural progression to lucid dreaming. One method of shamanic lucid dreaming is based on the understanding that you don't need to go to sleep in order to dream. The easiest way to become a conscious or lucid dreamer is to start out lucid and stay that way.

Australian author, historian and dream shaman Robert Moss wrote about shamanic dreaming:

> As dreamers, we are time travellers... Our ability to travel into the future is essential to our survival and well-being. We not only bring back memories of future events for which we - and sometimes whole communities - can then prepare. We visit possible futures, and our ability to read our memories of the possible future and then take appropriate action can determine whether we can escape a future event we don't like, or manifest one that we want.

WHAT IS SHAMANISM?

Shamanism is an earth-based wisdom system, the oldest mystic tradition found in indigenous tribes and cultures dating back over 40,000 years. It is believed to be humanity's most primal means of connecting with nature, creation and Mother Earth. Although most people associate Shamanism with Native American peoples, anthropologists have studied evidence of shaman practices on all continents going back to the Paleolithic era. Our ancestors practised Shamanism to celebrate the seasons, heal wounds and illnesses, find lost persons and objects, warn the tribe of dangers, ensure the success of the hunt, prevent tribal warfare and dream a new future for their community.

Essentially, Shamanism is a means by which humans have tried to understand the universe and their place in it. It does not force you to believe in any particular deity or dogma; what's important is the relationship with nature and using it for insight to heal physically, mentally and/or spiritually and to promote communal prosperity.

Although general shamanic practices include ceremony, dance, music, sweat lodges and entheogens (mind-altering substances), the heart of it is dreaming. A shaman can enter the dream world by shifting attention in a relaxed state and connect with spirits, ancestors and dream guides via methods such as breath control, fasting, sweats, solitary vision quests, dancing, chanting, some psychotropic substances, visualisation devices and the repetitive use of drumming.

The word 'shaman' comes from the Tungus of Siberia and is usually translated as 'one who sees in the dark' or 'one who is exalted or lifted up'. Shamans can be both male and female and are known as medicine men or women in most indigenous cultures The practices are usually led by a shaman, an oracle who has altered their consciousness to obtain knowledge from the spirit world and help bring healing to their community. A shaman is therefore a conduit or pathway to the spirit world.

A shaman is also a wounded healer. At some point in their lives they would have been badly wounded or ill and at the point of death, but they recovered and experienced a profound compassion for the suffering of others.

> A shaman's role is to walk on the edge of the known and unknown as a guide for their community and provide spaces for healing.

Spirituality and dream-work author Thomas Dale Cowan describes shamans as 'bridges who have relationships with the spirit worlds and carry life force between the ordinary and non ordinary realities'. The spirits can both be in animal form – coyote, bear, wolf, eagle, deer, crow, snake, giraffe, elephant – and human form – Archangel Michael, Merlin, Bridget, Buddha, Tara, Kuan Yin, Mary, White Buffalo Calf Woman – but whatever form they take they are there to provide guidance and assistance. Once the shaman has received the guidance they must journey back to ordinary reality and make use of it or apply it to situations. To do this in the dreaming world takes extensive training and practice.

I want to emphasise that nobody in the West apart from Celtic and other Europeans forms is a shaman in the typical meaning of the word. You have to have grown up in a spiritual culture of a particular lineage that is passed on to you, or you are chosen by the community or a spirit ancestor. It takes up to 20 years of training to become a tribal shaman and there are a number of casualties along the way due to its stressful nature. It's a difficult path with great responsibility. Although there are shamanic practitioners who call themselves modern shamans, they are not traditional shamans. You can learn some of the dreaming practices in a weekend, but it's only the very beginning of complex, lifelong lessons. Dreaming in the shamanic way is not a fad or a replacement for therapy, nor is it an escape from the day's pressures or about experiencing virtual pleasures. Rather, it is for journeying to meet up with your power animal, teacher or guide to ask for help at a time in your life when you want to make some serious life changes.

In dreaming the shaman becomes your dream guide in the hypnagogic state when you experience an altered state of consciousness and are ready to explore the worlds beyond your ordinary life. Modern shaman Sandra Ingerman says:

Shamanism teaches that there are doorways into other realms of reality where helping spirits reside who can share guidance, insight, and healing not just for ourselves but also for the world in which we live. It [shamanism] reveals that we are part of Nature and one with all life. Since we are part of nature, nature itself becomes a helping spirit that has much to share with us about how to bring our lives back into harmony and balance.

DREAMING IN THE SHAMANIC WAY

Shamans know that the non-ordinary reality of the world of hidden things is really a parallel universe to the one in which we live. Australian Indigenous people call the non-ordinary realms the Dreamtime; in Celtic traditions it is known as the Otherworld and as the spirit worlds by many indigenous peoples. One of the main differences between the hidden realities and our ordinary world is that they are inhabited by compassionate, helping spirits who offer guidance and healing on behalf of all life on earth. They may be seen as archetypal forces that indigenous peoples refer to as spirits, ancestors and gods.

What would your life be like if you believed your waking world was an extension of your dreaming world? In fact, most shamanic traditions such as the indigenous South American peoples believe that the dream world is the real world and the waking world is the dream world, that the everyday physical world came into being in response to the dream world and not vice versa. You could say that many people sleepwalk throughout their lives in an automated, programmed way without being truly awake to their individual nature and abilities.

Shamanic journeywork is a form of dreaming, although it is dreaming while awake (lucid dreaming). In a shamanic journey you might choose to go to any of the three worlds (the lower world, the middle world or the upper world; see further on in this chapter) to ask your helping spirits for healing and problem solving and receive answers. In your ordinary dreams at night you don't have that kind of conscious control, but in lucid dreaming you can direct your dreams.

Lucid dreaming is important to shamanic practitioners because it is a portal into other worlds. If you can control your dreams the portal can be accessed more directly, and a shaman can dream about which medicines are needed to heal people or what rituals need to be conducted for a bumper crop or to relieve drought. Your job as a lucid dreamer is to perceive the unseen powers behind the images in the natural world, which is filled with its own beauty; that is the first point of awareness. Try practising really seeing nature with its complexities and sacred geometry, its wildlife, oceans and natural wonders, with all of your five senses.

If you practise shamanic methods of living you will become familiar with lucid dreaming as a way of accessing the higher realms of consciousness. Dreaming is not just what happens during sleep but in the border state, the liminal state, between sleep and being awake. It is the place of ancient encounter with spiritual allies so it's essential you put yourself in that space to experience healing and dreams of a better future for yourself.

Dream shaman Robert Moss described the twilight state hypnagogia as 'a creative laboratory . . . a place of encounter . . . the best space to meet the gods'. He quoted Tinkerbell from *Peter Pan*: 'You know the place between sleep and awake, that place where you still remember dreaming . . . that's where I'll be waiting.' Dreaming your way out of this world and connecting with spiritual resources is practising dream yoga in a shamanic way. To navigate crises a shaman is a master dreamer, one who can visualise ways through in difficult times and put you in touch with your spiritual world. In shamanic dreaming you learn that your soul craves a deeper sense of purpose.

You can easily bring shamanic practices into your life by creating conscious dreaming experiences. This means you will be guided to:

- connect to nature spirits and animal spirits as your power animal
- connect to your tribal and ancestral lines on the spiritual plane via spirit guides and past lives
- journey to other non-worldly realities and dimensions
- channel energy and messages from the spirit world into this world
- practise soul retrieval and heal your inner child
- reach lucid states through the use of drums, repetitive sound, dance and song and safe medicinal herbs.

ANIMAL SPIRITS AND GUIDES

In shamanism, fields of intelligence take natural forms such as a tree spirit or a bear, which then offer the answers through the senses of the shaman. When shamans dream they are often accompanied by spirit allies that appear in animal form. A shaman develops a strong working connection with power animals, which then provide guidance and protection. If you have been led into a shamanic dream journey or have done your own visualisation meditation you may already be familiar with a power animal, or you may have met an animal guardian in a previous journey or your animal spirits may be looking for you in dreams and in nature – both in the waking and non-waking world. Once you make a connection with a power animal you can deepen and grow that connection by calling on them for healing, protection and help in your journey. In your waking life, you must honour your animal and nature spirits.

Note that there is a difference between a power animal and a totem animal. A power animal comes and goes, whereas a totem animal is constant and remains with you. You get the ones you need and your animal will have the medicine you require for healing. Only you will know what that is. When you're on a dream journey (such as a soul loss journey) you'll need a guide or animal to protect you. In this dream state, the higher you fly the more you need to be grounded by something familiar such as a power animal.

A power animal means a great deal to shamans, who are able to shape-shift into the form of an animal or bird familiar or to project a dream double in this form. Shamanic dreamers can replicate the dream body and send out doubles in different forms. Some dreamers can shape-shift into the shape of their power animals in their lucid dreams. When this happens, the dreamer is given a deep lesson and a gift to take back into their waking life.

I once entered a dream journey space with a visualisation and drumming that took me to a hypnagogic state where lucid dreaming was possible. It began with imagining I was in a natural environment – a meadow, forest, desert, waterway – and then looking around to see what was in that habitat. I waited for the power animal to look for me rather than looking for it myself, as is the case with visualisation. I saw tall trees and wondered what was behind them. I was open to whatever animal greeted me first and I would accept its gift.

I was hoping for the most desired power animals – jaguar, wolf, eagle – but instead a most unlikely and surprising guide appeared: a giraffe. What was its gift to me? What medicine did I need? I went through the process of understanding its lesson and these were my thoughts: *I need to stick my neck out more and not stay in my comfort zone; have a broader perspective; look at the bigger picture; I am above pettiness and small mindedness; cherry pick – be selective – with my time, friends, work; taste all there is (giraffes have long tongues); savour the moment; live in the present.*

What excellent medicine! My hypnagogic journey had manifested the perfect power animal for what was going on in my waking life. The adult giraffe has few natural predators, as its length, size and deadly kick protect it from lions, leopards and hyenas. These important details told me to live and let live and to have confidence in my own abilities. After I was back in my waking life I honoured the giraffe by bringing it into my reality. I looked for a wood carving of a giraffe in our local artisan store and found the perfect one. The idea is to 'feed' the power animal. Giving it my praise, thanks and honouring it by having it on my desk in my home office was my way of feeding it.

My next soul journey experience with a power animal was with a wolf. This was much more aligned with the typical shamanic animal kingdom and I felt ready for its strong energy. The message went something like this: you can be a member of the pack and survive, but there are pressures and you need to conform. You can survive being a lone wolf too, and that is your choice. More importantly, let go of the pack mentality. Each power or spirit animal is unique to the dreamer, but there are some important features that are shared in shamanic understanding of what these animals represent.

Crows and **ravens** are message bringers from the spirit world. The crow is a popular power animal and is revered as one of the sacred ancestors. For some Native Americans, Celts and Siberians the crow has mystical powers and was the creator of the visible world. The eye of the crow was thought to be the entrance to the supernatural realms, and it was believed that crows were shape-shifters with the ability to expand into other realms of consciousness. The special powers of the crow are its ability to be in two places at once; to take on other physical forms; to merge into the past, present and future; and to travel out of darkness into light. Crow medicine allows for healing at an unconscious level, disrupting and eliminating thought patterns as well as blocks at a cellular level. If you have the crow as your power animal be aware that great changes are coming and that you need to look deeper within and allow messages to come through from the mysterious inner realms.

Jaguars are a symbol of beauty, grace and the untamed feminine, awakening inner passions. No matter how difficult your life is there is always a promise of being led back to your true nature, but you must use your instincts and intuition. The jaguar was a sacred animal in pre-Columbian South and Central America; during religious rituals the people dressed in jaguar skins. The Mayan civilisation considered the jaguar an animal that enabled communication between the living and the dead.

Coyote energy is playful and is connected to trust and innocence. Coyotes are known to be tricksters, so the message of the coyote spirit animal may appear in the form of a joke or trickster. Adapting to new situations, not taking things too seriously and connecting to family are the hidden wisdoms of the coyote.

Wise **owls** are harbingers of change and messengers from beyond. They are powerful allies in the dream world. Owls can peer through the darkness and fly soundlessly through night skies, and owl medicine can reveal the unseen.

CELTIC SHAMANIC DREAMING

Nature spirits are as powerful as power animals in shamanic practices. Celtic shaman and author Jane Burns teaches that trees were the first shamans, that they taught humans how to be shamans and shared their wisdom and their medicine. The ancient Celts, especially the Druids, were forest people who loved their forests and trees and believed trees were grounding spirits with a connection to the heavens.

The ancient Celts created a sacred gathering place or circle called a *nemeton,* which were primarily natural clearings in the forest. They believed the trees had created the clearing because they recognised sacred ground. The opened canopy was a connection between the earth and spirit. The nemeton was viewed as a place of invocation, ceremony and creation – a place where heaven and earth united.

There is a special connection between trees and dreamers. Druids are known as 'those who see with the eyes of the oak'; oak is the most holy tree of the Druids. Many traditions used trees as symbols, representing qualities and ceremonial meanings. The mythological Yggdrasil, the sacred world tree of the Vikings, was an ash on which Odin hung for many days and nights to gain wisdom. Ash therefore represents mystical knowledge. As ancient peoples passed on the special attributes of the trees they gave an energetic signature that became tradition. Today these energies continue to be attributed to the trees in a shamanic (nature wisdom) way.

With meditation and drumming the shaman would step into the forest clearing, which would be encompassed by 13 trees.

The Celts believed that each tree has certain helpful characteristics or medicine and that it has a gift to offer us, as follows:

◎ alder: resilience and foresight

◎ apple: creativity, beauty, magic

◎ ash: unity, connection to the divine

◎ birch: clarity, cleansing, renewal

◎ blackthorn: transformation, change

◎ elder: rebirth, endings

◎ hawthorn: sanctuary, solitude

- hazel: wisdom, insight

- oak: strength, endurance

- rowan: protection, invincibility

- silver fir: far view, perspective

- willow: grace, release from sadness

- yew: deep inner peace, tranquillity.

You can visualise any tree, including these sacred trees, and make it your special tree in an inner sense, that is, for you to be aware of your mind's state of consciousness and to practise reflection as you take claim your tree. You can then return to it any time you choose in your dreaming state.

In *The Hidden Life of Trees,* author and forester Peter Wohlleben gives us a scientific explanation of the forest as a social network, describing how trees are able to communicate via electrical impulses that pass through the roots and also use the senses of smell and taste to warn other trees of predators and impending dangers. Like human families, trees are social: they take care of each other, they share nutrients and communicate that they need each other by offering support through the use of soil fungi that keeps them connected as part of an intimate network.

Estonia's holy forests are sacred sites to followers of the traditional forest religion of Maausk. *Maa* is Estonian for 'the land', so Maausk is sometimes translated as 'nature worship' or 'earth believer'. Generations have brought and some still do bring offerings into the forest. Maausk shrines in the forest are a reminder of indigenous forest worship similar to that of the Celtic Druids and the old Germanic religions before Christianity took hold. Its people have retained their deep and ancient connection to nature.

Ancient people knew that the trees and forests were essential to a healthy ecosystem of the earth – our lifeline and more alike than we could ever have imagined. Like a single tree, a single human is more vulnerable and has less chance of survival than when they are protected by the group (collective) or forest. The Celts praised and exulted the beauty of nature, and deeply observed and listened to it.

Celtic shamanic dream journeys, called *immrams,* took them to a place where the lines between matter and spirit blurred, a numinous space where mists descended, strange things happened and portals to other worlds opened. Known to them as the Otherworld, it is the place we know as the between and the betwixt, a world we can access through our dreams and be in contact with all that emanates from the non-material world. By letting go of the familiar, of what you think you know, and allowing for a numinous experience you become what is known in shamanic practice as a 'hollow bone'.

The Celts believed that the state of both the outer and inner worlds had to be in the right relationship with the earth, that humans needed to have respect and love with passion and willingness to serve the Great Mother of the land that gives life. The ancient Celts were willing to stand in alignment with the generous life-giving flow of the cycles of nature. Today, we are being called to action to revive and reconnect with the sacredness of Mother Earth.

When the bond between the people and the land is broken it creates a deep wounding and loss. Both the industrial revolution and mass migration from Europe to new lands such as Australia, the United States and Canada in the last 150 years still affect the ancestors of those who left their homeland as the land had been passed down from previous ancestors and there was a symbiotic relationship as a result of that bond.

Our dreams are hugely influenced by our sense of place, and the feelings connected to place and the world around us are key to well-being.

Dream teacher Toko-pa Turner says:

'We live in one of the most connected times on earth but never before have we been so lonely, so alienated from each other, from ourselves, and from the natural world. Whether this manifests as having difficulty finding community, feeling anxiety about your worthiness and place in the world, or simply feeling disconnected, the absence of belonging is the great silent wound of our times.'

Many of us feel displaced and cut off from our place of origin. We grieve by returning to the place we feel we belong in either physically or mentally in order to understand how it has shaped us. The point of dreams is to help us move forward. Shamanic practices that are based in an earth wisdom culture understand the disconnection and alienation that cause people to feel cut off, so shamans use visualisations and dream journeys to go into imaginal realms where we can create our own sense of place and belonging. The three-tiered cosmos of the shaman provides a sense of place as he journeys into worlds beyond the ordinary. You can also access this world by using your active imagination.

THE THREE WORLDS OF SHAMANISM

Australia's First Peoples believe we dream our way into the world and dream our way out of it. They look to dreams as the place of encounter with spiritual guides and sacred healers, who often appear as totem animals but may come in many other forms. Historian and author Robert Moss explains how among some traditions spirit men and clever men are called by dreams and serve their apprenticeship inside the dream world. Shamans are selected and made by ancestral spirits who appear to them in their dreams, and through the dreams teach the shamans important skills including the geography of the spirit worlds.

How is a shamanic state of consciousness achieved when the shaman is not in a sleep state? All shamans use a form of monotonous, repetitive percussion such as drumming or rattling to achieve an altered state in which visionary experience become accessible. Robert Moss says shamanic drumming 'quietens the monkey mind and helps you focus so you can override old mental patterns. Some believe that shamanic drumming may harmonise neural activity in the brain with the frequency of the beat.' In the deep, reflective dream-like theta state, a visionary experience can be achieved. The theta state is 'below' the alpha state (when we are in an awake state) and 'above' the delta state (when we are asleep and dreaming). This in-between zone is where our brain normally fires nerve impulses between 4 and 7 Hz.

Shamans go into a cosmology of three worlds when they channel and ask spirit to move through them into the ordinary world so their wisdom can be accessed.

The three-levelled world system (cosmology) of non-ordinary reality is the shamanic dream world. It is made up of the upper, middle and lower worlds. Shamans may travel to any of the three worlds in order to, for instance, contact a spiritual teacher from the upper world or meet a power animal ally in the middle world to bring back songs from the rocks, rivers, mountains and stars. Although the three worlds have numerous levels within each world, for ease I have used the collective word 'world' to describe them.

THE LOWER WORLD

The lower world is formed by the spirits of nature: the spirits of animals, trees, plants, rocks and mythical creatures such as dragons and unicorns. Trees are seen as being guardian spirits. It is the home of various helper spirits such as power animals, which can become protectors of the shamanic dreamer. The lower world is where the shaman journeys to connect with the spirit of the wolf, bear, raven or tiger, healing herbs, oak or corn or even with elementals: the spirits of fire, water, earth or stone. Many of these spirits are willing to come into relationship with humans as spirit helpers, providing us with protection and support and with the benefit of the powers they possess.

THE MIDDLE WORLD

The middle world has two aspects: an ordinary physical aspect and a non-ordinary dream aspect. It is the place of human dreaming and the one in which you live in your day-to-day life. When you lucid dream, journeying to the middle world is essentially astral projection as your light body leaves your physical body and you can travel around the world at the speed of thought, as well as back or ahead in time. The middle world has other worlds within it that include all realms where time and space exist. It can be accessed through journeying and is often the destination for soul retrieval and for seeing things from the past, although it requires a great deal of skill to journey there.

The non-ordinary aspect of the middle world is where you will find yourself immediately after the death experience. It is the bardo state of the Tibetans and the purgatory of Judeo-Christianity, regions populated largely by the souls of recently deceased humans. The modern mystic Robert Monroe calls this place 'The Park', a waiting place where you get used to your new non-physical body state and where you undertake a life review. A life review is where in the bardo states the soul has to relive all the pain they have caused in their lifetime, the persons they hurt and the pain of all the relatives. Many who experience a near-death experience confirm this.

The Tibetan Book of the Dead (the Bardo Thodol) reveals that when we die it's like going into a dream and not waking up. The dream we go into is our own unique dream, one we create for ourselves during our soul's transition from the physical world into the dreaming of the spiritual world. According to shaman Sandra Ingerman, these post-mortem dreams (bardos) are in-between states that last for around 40 days. Long prayers are recited over the deceased for the full 40 days in order to remind the discarnate soul that all they are experiencing in the bardos are illusions and dreams.

During this period the discarnate soul may be approached by many spirits, including spirit guides, and with the life review accomplished the deceased soul becomes a soul sprit and ascends with the higher spirits into the upper world (heaven in Judeo-Christianity and paradise in Islam). Here the soul re-emerges with its source and becomes one again with its higher self or oversoul. A shaman can travel in the middle worlds and find the souls of the recently deceased in order to help them cross to the afterlife. It is in the middle world they can look for lost objects, and perform remote healing work.

The middle world is inhabited by a variety of spirits some refer to as the hidden fold: the fairies, elementals and forest guardians who once existed in a time before the veils between the worlds closed. A shaman can communicate with the spirits contained in all the things that live in our existing physical world such as rocks, water and plants.

THE UPPER WORLD

The upper world is formed by the collective dreaming of the gods, goddesses, angelic forces and spiritual heroes and heroines of the past. There, through this very expanded dream world, you may find connection with your spirit guides, ascended masters and members of your council or elder spirits. Shamans believe that our spirit guides serve as spiritual teachers, and that it is through them we have a very special connection with our personal oversoul. A shaman may journey into the upper world in search of a person's missing soul (see the section later in this chapter on soul retrieval). They can help a person become whole again after accidents or trauma and can cure illness and other misfortune.

The upper world has many layers: it is the wider universe, the heavens and planes of higher consciousness. As your etheric body moves outside your physical body when you astral travel the upper world should only be accessed if you are a shaman or an experienced shamanic dreamer.

During an out-of-body experience the astral body gathers memories and experience, and the dream mind becomes active. There are three versions of 'you' – the physical, astral and dream – and each version has three separate memory streams. When you wake up you will have random memory pieces. You may have multiple dreams in the many upper world realms; safely navigating the different levels and returning with gifts for this world. This requires practise and discipline.

There may be six to 10 levels in dreams that are out of physical reality. Strong memories can be created through fear, so you will likely experience lucid nightmares and sleep paralysis. Anthropologist Guy Mount interviewed a Cahuilla medicine woman, Ruby Modesto, who shared her experience in multi-levelled dreaming. When she was young she dreamed to the 13th level but did not know how to come back:

> I kept having different dreams and falling asleep [inside each level of dreaming] and going to another level. In the course of this immense, multi-tiered experience Ruby met her shamanic ally, Ahswit the eagle, but her spirit was lost in the dreamlands. For days she was semi-comatose in a sleep from which no one could rouse her. Her father tried to bring her back to her body but couldn't. Finally, Uncle Charlie, a specialist in soul retrieval, was able to find her spirit and put it back in her body. Ruby said: 'When I woke up they made me promise not to dream like that again, not until I knew how to get back by myself.'

When the astral body wants to come back into the sleeping body it must be in the process of waking. Some dreamers have described the astral body as feeling wet and clammy, as though it were covered with ectoplasm.

Upper world journeys can provide great insights into your life path and personal growth that can be utilised in your waking life, but it takes a great deal of energy and mind control of your sleeping body states to be able to achieve this. If you manage to reach the shamanic upper worlds you may find a benevolent spiritual teacher who has been looking out for your well-being since you were born.

Depending on your level of commitment to the dream world, you can enter the three worlds as a conscious dreamer in the sense that you know dreaming is not just recreational but comes from a sacred space. A dream or visualisation can be a portal to any of the many worlds within the three worlds, to places of healing, initiation and adventure including those in which you can meet people who have passed on, ancestors, your power animal guide or nature spirit guide and higher beings. To achieve the shaman's dream power it is necessary to be able to dream strong, to be committed to the practices of dreaming and then allow yourself to travel within the dream and find healing.

SHAMANIC DREAM JOURNEYING TECHNIQUES

Some of the techniques for beginning journeyers is to find a visual focus for entry into one or more of the three worlds.

To enter the lower world and make a connection with a helping spirit such as a power animal you may visualise a tunnel or burrow leading down deep into the earth, or entering a cave or body of water such as lake or river, a tree trunk or a volcano. You just need to know that this place exists in reality even if you have not been in it. Follow the tunnel and then into the light, repeating the intention: *'I wish to meet a spirit helper.'* When you open your eyes you should find something or someone waiting for you; if it's your power animal, ask your questions.

To travel in the middle world (the non-ordinary part of our world) you may be familiar with the landscape, one in which you can communicate with nature, visit people at a distance, search for something that's missing and scout your future. You may visualise walking out of your front door or stepping out of your car and travelling to some place where you feel comfortable, such as a garden. This is an exciting world to visit as it gives you access to faeries and elementals (spirit people) along with as the entire solar system.

To rise up to the upper world to find a teacher or spirit guide you can use your imagination to visualise something high such as being on top of a mountain, climbing a rope or a tree, flying up in a tornado like Dorothy in *The Wizard of Oz* or even finding a bird to take you up. The key focus is the upward movement. If you're more adventurous you could visualise upward travel in a hot air balloon. Some shamans use the tree of life and journey down the roots into the lower world or up the trunk into the branches to travel into the upper world. You may travel through the other two worlds to get to the upper world, but keep focusing on your intention to meet a spirit teacher. You may even meet your higher self or oversoul.

The specific things shamans encounter in their journeys are unique for each individual and each trip; this will be the same for you as a conscious dreamer in the three worlds. Like the shaman, the more you practise the more you will be able to build a mental map of the alternate reality you are entering, which will allow you to better understand and use the knowledge you gain in a practical way.

To go on to dream journey to any of the three worlds you will need to find appropriate drumming music. In *Cave and Cosmos*, researcher Michael Harner claims the most widespread element in shamanic rituals is a drum beat at approximately four beats per second, which induces a synchronisation of brain waves conducive to trance states. You may want to find a shamanic practitioner or someone who has experience in this practice to guide you if you are not confident about doing it alone. However, visualisations are about active imagination – something that can be done by anyone at any time – and that is what's needed when you lucid dream. Guided meditation, mindfulness and breathwork are great aids for dream journeying.

There are more advanced techniques available, but here are some basic guidelines to shamanic dream journeying:

Prepare: choose a place where you will be undisturbed for half an hour. You will need a device and headphones with which you can listen to drumming. Make yourself comfortable in any position that you like. Clear the space with palo santo or sage and call in protection from your guides or guiding spirits.

Choose your intention: for each journey you need to have a clear intention. What is it you want out of this experience: advice, healing, excitement? You may want some clarity around an issue such as a relationship or your work. Questions might include 'What do I need to focus on in my life right now that will help me grow?' As a beginner, you may wish to get to know this non-ordinary reality by simply exploring it the first few times.

Choose your world: think of an actual location that you've visited or one you can remember from a photo, image or video or other personal source; your mind needs to have a clear image. Choose which world you want to enter then see above for a suitable portal of entry to it. Use just one entrance for the upper world and one for the lower world so you can build a location map in the non-ordinary world.

Begin your journey: start with a relaxed mind. Turn on the drumming music, close your eyes and repeat the intention: *'I want to explore the lower world.'* If you choose this alternate reality, visualise and feel yourself being at the tunnel entrance or burrow into the earth. Once you have gone through the portal, follow it to explore the spaces your mind imagines.

The return: when you are ready to return, reverse your tracks through the portal up to the place you first started to imagine; it will be at a quicker pace than when you entered.

Journalling and rituals: write down your experience in detail once you are back in the ordinary world. Create a ritual around it with a physical manifestation of the message from the dream journey.

Purpose: a shaman's ultimate purpose is to heal and help others. Whether you want to do this or just to use it as part of your own personal development, your first step should be to learn to help yourself and accumulate knowledge of the non-ordinary reality.

SOUL RETRIEVAL

A major contribution of the shamans to healing today is their practice of soul retrieval when we suffer soul loss. The loss of life force, of our vital energy and identity is known as 'soul loss'. In order to be whole and well, the shaman must find the means of soul recovery known as 'soul retrieval'.

Soul loss occurs when you undergo emotional and physical trauma, a separation, grief or a series of difficult circumstances and part of your life force retracts so your body and consciousness can survive whatever is happening to you. In this state you are operating in a weakened state of incompleteness, much like when we are convalescing. Also known as 'disassociation', it is a splintering from big emotional intensity until further notice.

Along with the tracking and recovery of lost soul fragments, soul retrieval involves the restoration of vital energy and wholeness to the lost parts. The purpose of soul retrieval is to return a part of a person's soul or spirit to its rightful place. However, problems develop when the soul fragments become lost and are unable or unwilling to return, which can result in depression, illness, addictions and post-traumatic stress syndrome. A shaman will track the parts of the soul that have fled and recover them in a soul retrieval ceremony. By restoring a lost piece of the soul to where it belongs the shaman facilitates the healing process and the recipient begins to feel stronger and more whole.

In traumatic situations the soul part may not return to the body on its own and may need outside support to return the soul essence. In indigenous cultures, the lost soul part is a separated spirit being that often takes the form of a child or adult at the age when the traumatic splitting occurred. These partial souls that were split continue to exist in the spirit worlds, so a shaman must journey into the three worlds to find and persuade the lost soul parts to return home.

The rhythmic beating of a drum takes the shaman into an altered state of consciousness, the same way we enter our dreaming state, and in spirit flight into any or all of the three mysterious worlds to meet with helping spirits, power animals, ancestors or spirit guides. The shaman may journey outside of linear time altogether and go to the place where the traumatic event is still occurring for a person (a parallel universe), locate the person's missing life force and restore it. The soul is then sung back home, blown into the body of the recipient and given a welcome home ceremony. Once returned, the soul parts are nurtured and integrated so that healing can begin. All shamanic healing is considered to be a gift from the helping spirits.

After soul retrieval a person will experience changes, for some quite subtle changes while for others they are sudden and visibly evident. When welcomed and sung home the return of a person's soul may bring back more vitality and a sense of purpose, to help break old patterns and open up new possibilities for more positive life changes.

SYMPTOMS OF SOUL LOSS

The most common cause of soul loss occurs when you have suffered a trauma or a chronic illness in your life and you become disassociated from yourself. A number of other symptoms are associated with soul loss, including:

- feeling incomplete, fragmented or outside of your body
- addictions
- chronic depression, feeling suicidal
- PTSD
- ongoing grief and difficulty moving on after loss, separation, divorce or the death of a loved one

- ◎ immune deficiency

- ◎ apathy, feeling numb or a lack of direction

- ◎ being stuck in a recurring pattern

- ◎ wanting to engage less with the world around you or observing life as an outside

- ◎ feeling spaced out and not present

- ◎ an inability to trust.

There are other, more subtle characteristics of soul loss that are not obvious and may be overlooked. Soul loss can simply feel like a longing, of feeling homesick in some way or that you don't belong. You might have left your childhood town, your country of origin or other physical place that is meaningful to you and consequently feel displaced, that the good energy you felt when you were in these places has been lost somewhere. You might be feeling that something is missing in your marriage, job or relationship because you are staying longer than necessary. You might notice symptoms of sadness, guilt, fatigue, low energy, an absence of dream recall, recurring dreams, low self-esteem or not letting go of someone or something even if they are no longer in your life.

You will find that you want to fill the void from soul loss with distractions and excuses not to travel to the imaginary worlds the shamans go into. In order to be able to find and retrieve your lost parts you will need to let go of something.

Through conscious dreaming we can retrieve and restore lost parts of ourselves. Our dreams offer us maps we can use to travel to the places where our soul was lost and can be found and brought home. We can find our ancestors and spirit guides in our dreams, as they come searching for us in our dreams. This conscious connection will allow us to begin the healing process and open the way for recovery at a cultural soul and collective level.

It sometimes happens that prolific dreamers one day suddenly stop dreaming or have a dream drought for months, and I have been asked a number of times why we lose our dreams. There is no one answer that fits this phenomenon, but in shamanic belief if you've lost your dream recall you've lost your soul. A recurring dream is also an indication of soul loss. If you believe in the metaphysical 'as within, so without' principle you need to look at your waking world. Have you stopped consciously dreaming your inner dreams? Have you forgotten dreams of what it is you want to do? All of your ambitions, hopes and achievements have been forgotten and are no longer visible. The bright dreamer in you and the vitality that lives in your soul have gone away, lost in the three upper worlds of the shaman.

Think about the last dream you had that had potency, and imagine yourself stepping back into that dream as an older version of yourself. When you connect with your younger self a new dreamer will come back. Imagine as a time traveller you can journey to your younger self and provide the comfort, support and encouragement desperately needed in that timeframe. You might say something like: 'I promise that you will get through this.' By becoming a friend to your younger self, healing can take place in the present time and also for you in the past time.

SIGNS

Some shamans believe that whatever happens in waking life has already been dreamed before, except the dreamer had not been looking at the signs. The world speaks to you in the same way a dream does via symbols and signs, and a shaman will teach you to pay close attention to the symbolic meanings of events and patterns in your waking life. There are no coincidences, only synchronicity. The tools of divination are at your disposal on a daily basis: in the chance encounter, the flight of birds, the sudden appearance of a power animal, a conversation overhead in a café. If these signs are the answers, what is the question? During your waking hours, practise looking around you and seeing everything as a dream symbol. Remind yourself often that what you seem to be taking for reality is actually a very detailed dream. Simply changing your perspective will be enough to affect many of the habits and patterns you want to change.

Part of being a shamanic dreamer is finding your question and putting it out into the world. Carry it with you everywhere you go, then look for the answer through signs around you both in your waking world and in your dream world. If you invite synchronicity, signs and symbols into your ordinary life it will be easier to encounter them in your lucid dream state, where answers may be gifted to you.

Symbols and signs are the language your spirit self uses, and are largely confined to the subconscious mind. Shamans make it a point to take charge of the subconscious and make it conscious, so they learn to direct symbols and utilise them.

DREAM RITUALS AND PRACTICES

You can learn how to ask for help in your night-time dreams just as you do in setting an intention for a shamanic journey.

FOR GUIDANCE

◎ When you begin a new project or need advice, simply ask for a dream to provide you with guidance. Before you go to sleep at night set an intention that you would like to receive helpful advice in a dream. This is also known as dream incubation.

◎ Write down a dream you have received that gives you guidance. Sometimes the answer will be clear but sometimes you will have to sit with the message, figuring out how the symbols or message answer the intention you set for your dream.

◎ Dreams can help you solve major dilemmas, as they can bring on healing even on the physical level. A helping spirit may appear in your dream and offer healing, or an unknown being may come to offer help.

◎ Ask for help for your own personal burdens and also ask for spiritual guidance for your ancestors.

FOR COMMUNICATION

Rituals and ceremony are essential and vital parts of shamanic practices. Create a space and allow spirit to communicate with you, then you may wish to add any or all of these rituals:

◎ Light a candle and breathe in and out into the flame, allowing yourself to become the flame. This will allow you to enter a light trance, and in that twilight state you can communicate best with the spirit world.

◎ Listen to drumming sounds to alter your conscious state and enter into the shamanic world of journeying.

- ◎ Burn incense and allow your senses to be activated. What does it smell like? If you imagine you are part of the smoke it will also induce a trance-like state.

- ◎ Allow a golden light to enter and clean your whole body and ask to remove any obstacles in your life.

FOR SHARING

It is vital for indigenous communities to share dreams, as it is beneficial for the dreamer and also for the group as it may shed light on situations that affect both individuals and the larger community in an interplay of symbols, visions and future well-being. Similarly, in dream groups different participants have dreams that overlap in meaning and have relevance to the entire circle, not just to the individual of the dream.

One dream-work process developed by Jungian therapist Montague Ullman has been successfully used with drumming as a shamanic adaptation. Each group member imagines a dream that somebody in the group has shared as their own dream and tries to interpret its message for themselves, rather than for the original dreamer. Rather than passing on judgement about the dream or saying what the dream means for the dreamer they begin by saying 'If it were my dream . . .' and say what it brings up for them as the listener. This allows everyone to gain a personal insight from the dream discussed into other aspects of their lives.

WHAT THE SHAMANS SAY

There is no better time than *now* to reflect on humanity's existence and connection to Mother Earth. Our deepest fear is our loss of connection to the planet and all her creatures, the great web of life and energy that we are part of. Shamanism is the most ancient spiritual practice that teaches we are one with all of life, yet we no longer understand this in our treatment of the earth. In metaphysical terms it's a matter of 'as within, so without', and the result can be equally damaging to our dream world. Indigenous peoples have known about the importance of a strong connection with earth energy for millennia; their ancient earth wisdom makes them caretakers of the land that sustains them.

One way to use your dreams to reconnect at a collective level to Mother Earth is through deep listening. For the First Nation peoples of Australia this is known as *dadirri,* which means 'deep listening', 'quiet' and 'still awareness'. It is a tuning-in experience with the focus on a deeper understanding of the beauty of nature and has been practised by Indigenous people for over 40,000 years.

Paying attention to what is around you in the natural world is as important as taking care of your dreaming life, which sustains you and keeps you in balance. Anthropologist and shaman Alberto Villoldo emphasises the importance of being a caretaker of the earth and of shamanic practices that are grounded in the natural world: 'To ground solidly, we need to create a framework within which we can relate to the world. Generally, this is based on the properties of the four cardinal and non-cardinal points of the compass, relating these to the four elements and other natural phenomena in the medicine wheel.'

Villoldo recommends we repair the past by shedding all of the structures and paradigms that no longer serve humanity, such as '. . . stories around masculine predatory mythology and relationship of abuse and of the matricide we are committing with Mother Earth'. He believes these structures must be put in a fire to release the life that is bound to them:

'Shamans used to heal themselves by releasing a death arrow or a stick in the fire . . . In the death arrow, mentally put in all that is no longer living, no longer sustainable and no longer life giving.' Fire is a great purifier with transformative powers; think of the phoenix. If we put our past stories in the fire we become an empty vessel of that experience and can reach out for a new vessel, and have an opportunity to reinvent ourselves at a collective level.

Mayan prophecies predicted the first humans would appear on the planet on 21 December 2012. These were the first rays of humanity, of the true humans, those who were capable of becoming. Many modern indigenous cultures believe we are the new humanity the Mayans referred to, that we are the new vessel. In releasing bondage to the past we can embrace what we are becoming.

Mystic author Caroline Myss believes we are all one huge organism, a micro planet: 'The rules of the planet have changed . . . all organs have to get along for survival. We are not separate. Mind, body, spirit is one system.'

The International Council of Thirteen Indigenous Grandmothers was formed when the grandmothers came together in 2004 from the four directions of the earth for the first time, 'uniting their diverse spiritual and cultural lineages to form a global alliance of prayer, as well as spiritual and environmental activism'. Grandmother Agnes Baker Pilgrim said: 'As humans we need to do a better job. Our job is to keep on doing good, not only for those who are alive on the planet, but also for the seven generations ahead.' In other words, the grandmothers are telling us loud and clear that there is no planet B.

The Hopi have always had their fingers on the pulse of the planet. They want to know if we are going through a portal or down a hole during the current times of social unrest and climate change. White Eagle from the Hopi tribe says:

This moment humanity is going through can now be seen as a portal and as a hole. The decision to fall into the hole or go through the portal is up to you. If you repent of the problem and consume the news 24 hours a day, with little energy, nervous all the time, with pessimism, you will fall into the hole. But if you take this opportunity to look at yourself, rethink life and death, take care of yourself and others, you will cross the portal.

In order to dream in a way that embodies the shamanic spirit of living in balance with nature we may have to become a shaman of our own soul and healer of our own lives. If the world around us is indeed a waking dream in the shamanic belief system then we will need to dream the future. Before we can do this we must follow the shaman's way and retrieve parts of our lost soul so we can recover those aspects of ourselves that need to be healed – not just at a personal level, but at a collective one.

You can do this in your sleep dreaming, in your awakened conscious dreaming state and in your synchronistic moments when you see signs all around you. Your imaginal worlds can mirror the shaman's three worlds, where you can imagine a new way of being in the world as a new vessel, a new humanity. *It starts with dreaming it first.* If enough of us transform we can re-imagine our world and leave the planet in a very different state from the one we have.

'Seeing' and 'being' the future are what our ancestors knew to be possible.

NATURE WALK

We are connected to the seasons and the five elements. Allow yourself to connect to nature's healing process: be present; go out in nature daily; sit and listen to the sounds around you. A one-minute daily practice a day will help you to connect to the spirits of nature, your ancestors and universal consciousness. Create space and allow spirit to communicate with you.

TREE GROUNDING

At a deeper meditative level you can use tree-grounding practices to bring balance and calm into your life and as a prompt to enter a lucid dream state before going to sleep. Trees are used as dream gates, as nature-based autosuggestions to enable you to enter a hypnagogic state. This can be done anywhere as it uses your active imagination to enter a daydream state of visualisation.

With your feet on the ground, take deep breaths until you feel calm. Reach down to the soles of your feet and feel your connection with the deep earth below you. Breathing in, let the energy of the earth rise up through the soles of your feet, then allow it to rise through your body all the way up to the crown of your head. See it returning to the earth like tiny atoms of life.

Now that you have earth energy within you, think of a favourite or significant tree; you may simply imagine a tree that appears to you. Imagine roots, as if your body is that tree. You have become one with the tree. Let your legs and the soles of your feet go deep into the soil as if they are the roots of a tree. You may notice you have very thick roots that firmly pull you down, which may be the thick roots of an oak that stands tall and strong, connecting you to the energy and strength of the earth. Do you have thinner roots of the elegant silver birch? Maybe your roots spread out to cover more area for greater balance and security.

Breathe up through the roots by moving your breath from the soles of your feet up through your calves and thighs, then through your legs up to the core of your body. Allow your tree to grow through your ribs and shoulders. Remember you are the tree. Feel the air as it moves through your branches and as it rustles the leaves. Feel the breath in your throat and let it expand into your head, relaxing your forehead and thoughts.

With each breath, imagine you are extending the roots up to the crown of your head. Feel your energy move from the soles of your feet up through your head and into the sky. Feel how your arms spread far and wide while reaching for the sky. The light filters through your canopy; birds rest on your branches; you feed on the sunshine and your breath becomes the lungs of the world.

With each in breath notice the cleansing energy, and with the out breath release all tension. Allow yourself to feel your body filling the expanse between earth and sky. Relax and continue to breathe in deep from your roots, from the soles of your feet. Allow this energy to spread throughout your body and release it from the crown of your head.

When you are ready, shift your awareness back to your feet and notice how the ground feels beneath your feet. Your connection to the rich earth and strong roots has provided you with energy and tranquillity. If you can find the tree you saw in your vision, find time to sit with it and listen to what wisdom it offers.

DREAMS
TAKE YOU
FROM
A BETA
STATE TO
AN EVEN
BETTER
STATE.

DREAMING IN MULTIPLE DIMENSIONS

'We are not human beings having a
spiritual experience; we are spiritual
beings having a human experience.'

– PHILOSOPHER PIERRE TEILHARD DE CHARDIN

ncient cultures regarded dreams and synchronicities as being more important than physical reality. Our collective dreams and synchronicities tap into consciousnesss; according to human consciousness author Anthony Peake, we are all 'one consciousness experiencing ourselves subjectively'.

The collective identity we have as part of humanity matters. Our actions have impacts on others: other consciousnesses, other existences and, of course, nature, and this connectivity shows we are not separate. Quantum science reveals that the physical reality we think is solid and material actually isn't. We are a wave on the ocean of consciousness and are all part of the same thing; that is, we are the part of the 'one drop of the ocean makes a whole ocean' theory. We all affect each other – in the physical and in the non-physical.

Previous chapters looked at ways to transcend beyond your reality, your fears and your patterns of behaviour. They showed how in the collective unconscious you are able to get a glimpse into your personal unconscious and discover through archetypes in the hero's journey how to face your shadow side. In lucid and shamanic dreams you discovered how to communicate with your animal and spirit guides and deceased ancestors.

This chapter outlines the theories around non-rational phenomena that affect your mind states and which relate to your dreaming states. When your conscious mind can't wrap itself around concepts such as precognitive dreams, near-death experiences, spirit guides, parallel universes, déjà vu and non-linear time, and the subconscious mind is not awakened to past lives, psychopomps, the afterlife and the Akashic records, there is one other mind that is across all of these concepts: the super conscious.

You can learn to access the full span of possibilities in your dreaming world, the state where you become an active dreamer and enter the portal within your higher self to a deeper spiritual awakening. It is the place for soul work, healing and transformation. There are other means of accessing your soul's wisdom, such as visualisations; however, if you can first glean information from your dreaming world then you have the key to delving further beyond the physical realm of understanding.

Your dreaming world gives you the ability to access a fuller range of consciousness beyond your conscious state of the five senses as there is a suspension of the ego's typical critical nature. Being more spiritually open is easier in your dreaming state, which is where you can engage in more complex dreaming practices that are ancient and have been utilised since early earth wisdom-based traditions. This deeper awakening can assist you with opening up to wisdom and clarity in your waking life.

To understand your own individual consciousness, one that taps into a universal consciousness, it's essential that you understand the three minds – the conscious, the subconscious and super conscious – and their functions.

THE CONSCIOUS, SUBCONSCIOUS AND SUPER CONSCIOUS MINDS

It's important to make a distinction between the mind and consciousness. The mind is an organism that reasons, thinks, feels, perceives and judges as well as having other specific mental functions and properties. Consciousness, however, has been defined as an awareness, a subjectivity and ability to experience a sense of self. Consciousness is in everything: it is a vibrating, expanding field of information that exists as infinite pure potential and hums with change and future possibility.

The mind is split into the conscious, the subconscious and the super conscious. You will be most familiar with the conscious mind, what you operate with in the physical world during your waking hours. It is a finite world that represents only a small portion of your awareness and is ruled by the five senses of sight, hearing, smell, touch and taste.

The subconscious mind lies below the level of conscious awareness recording everything you do, your likes and dislikes and your feelings and emotions, and for the most part remaining hidden from your conscious mind or everyday awareness. It is a very powerful influencer on how you act and think in the conscious state and, more significantly, how it reveals itself in your dreams. You dream within the subconscious mind, which is why some people believe this is where the inner self or the inner you resides. It was previously discussed in the book about how the images, emotions and scenarios that come up in dreams are those that are noted in the conscious mind but are not expressed in waking life. They are hidden from you until you re-awaken those experiences in dreams from the subconscious mind.

The super conscious is where you find creative ideas for great works of art, music, literature, poetry and inventions, as well as deep spiritual experiences. It is sometimes described as being where you come into direct contact with your higher self, soul, the universal mind or consciousness, infinite intelligence or wholeness/ oneness, which is the union of all selves. The super conscious mind understands that everything is made of energy and consciousness, that is, it has an awareness at a universal level that extends beyond your birth and death.

You are able to access the super conscious mind through spiritual, precognitive and prophetic dreams. Super conscious dreams will have a life-changing effect on you; they are known as numinous or 'big' dreams. The 'unexplained' belongs in the super conscious mind space. You need to stretch your conscious mind to embrace this concept with an aware and awakened mind. Finding unexplained phenomena in the unconscious or subconscious minds is not new; many experience this in the lucid dream state when they travel to other dimensions and levels of consciousness.

Some noteworthy and famous historical figures whose work has been much documented and referenced contributed to human advancement via dream awareness and altered states of highly developed consciousness. Their stories are outlined below.

EDGAR CAYCE: THE SLEEPING PROPHET

Edgar Cayce (1877–1945) is a well-known dreamer extraordinaire with a massive documented archive of dream experiences and thousands of dream-style, trance-like readings through his career that were scribed and recorded by his assistant. He has been referred to as the 'sleeping prophet' and the 'father of modern holistic medicine' due to his phenomenal ability to induce an altered state of consciousness similar to self-hypnosis to receive and retrieve information beyond the known world. The concept of 'trance' as referred to in relation to Cayce refers to an out-of-body experience, hypnotism or an altered state of awareness; it was known in religious circle as 'ecstasy'.

As a child Cayce claimed to have a vivid dream life and the ability to absorb information from books by sleeping with them under his pillow. When he woke up he would have literally and academically retained the knowledge within the text. He also stated he had regular in-depth communications with his deceased grandfather both in wakeful and sleeping hours, but especially during daydream experiences. Cayce's claims were not widely believed at the time, yet he was adamant about his experiences and had clients visit from far and wide to seek his help with their health issues. He was able to access medical guidance in his trance-style sleep and provide incredible accurate and medically precise details. Today he would be called a 'medical intuitive'.

Cayce said he was able to access the universal consciousness with universal intelligence (the super conscious), which provided the wisdom and insights he sought. Although recall is difficult from a trance state, he did retain the information and made sure his assistant documented it as soon as he returned to physical consciousness.

Cayce made numerous predictions about the future, some of which did not eventuate or haven't to date although they appear to be too accurate to dismiss out of hand. The predictions that did eventuate included: the 1925 stock market crash and the bigger 1929 major market crash; a second world war involving Austria, Germany and Japan (Cayce reported this in 1935, four years prior to the start of World War 2); the finding of the ancient Dead Sea Scrolls; a global communication merger (the internet, reported near the turn of the 20th century); and that blood would be used as a diagnostic tool for science and medicine. As the sleeping prophet we have to assume the details, insights and prophecies Cayce received in his altered state of dreaming came from the super conscious.

The following dream from 2012 mirrors Cayce's method of healing during a dream state. The dreamer, Anne, performed a distance healing in her lucid dream state. Distant healing dreams are similar to a shaman's soul retrieval practice of finding the correct medicine or healing for the patient (see Chapter 7 for more information).

I had been attending classes for a diploma of kinesiology and had a very rewarding and surprisingly successful day learning new knowledge on realigning anatomical posture. As I was leaving the campus for the day I had a friendly peer express her desire that I work on her left shoulder, which was one to two inches lower than her right shoulder and how it made her feel lopsided. I'd been having many dreams and practising healing and corrections on myself in my sleep, and would wake holding acupressure points or activating and directing energies that I had been learning about both in class and in my private interests of study consecutively.

I went to sleep that night and in one of my dreams I dreamt that I was in class. I noticed in my dream that I was conscious that I was dreaming. I had been practicing lucidity in my sleeping dream experiences and decided to check that I was actually in a dream. I was dreaming that I had just arrived at the college and was entering the classroom. On entry I paused at the doorway and attempted to switch the light off and on, which I could not: the lighting would not dim or change. This was my awareness that I was dreaming with a level of control and an indication that I was in a lucid state, therefore it confirmed by conscious awareness in my dream that I was having a lucid dream.

I entered the classroom, which was very bright, almost glowing, and then I saw my peer who has requested me to work on her shoulder. She looked twisted and very uneven in her postural composure as she approached me. We did not speak with our mouths at all yet had a telepathic dialogue in which she stated a desire for me to fix her uneven shoulder, as she knew I could.

In my lucid dream state I had no doubt of her request and began the protocol for correction. She lay on the healing table and I proceeded to test muscles and neurological patterns held within her body. I then performed the necessary corrections and she stood up from the table with even shoulders and an essence of relief with ease and joy; she was glowing and smiling radiantly. I awoke and thought: I didn't get to work with her on her shoulder yesterday yet at least I did in my dream.

I went to class and saw my peer standing in sunshine on the steps in front of the college. She was radiant, she seemed taller and her shoulders were not lopsided. She told me that she woke up and felt like I had worked on her overnight and asked if I had done a distance healing to fix her shoulder. I told her that I didn't do it while I was awake but that she presented in a dream I had where I was consciously controlling the scene and proceeded to perform a correction on her posture. I also told her I was totally elated and warmed to see her so vibrant and illuminated and had the postural alignment I had experienced within the actions in my lucid dream. The reality of seeing the results seemed dreamlike. The dream was reality.

NIKOLA TESLA: THE GENIUS INVENTOR

Nikola Tesla (1856–1943) was an inventor, engineer and futurist who utilised access to the collective consciousness and knowledge beyond the human realm of existential awareness. Like Cayce, as a child Tesla could memorise entire books and store logarithmic tables in his brain. He also easily picked up languages, and could work through days and nights on only a few hours sleep. In his adult years he had a series of daydreams, night dreams and lucid dreams and was said to have access to higher dimensions, from where he was able to receive instruction and detailed information about inventions in the fields of electricity and electrical engineering.

Tesla claimed to have gained knowledge and wisdom from both his wakeful daydream-like trances and in sleeping dream states. He reportedly invented over 12,000 devices, electrical conduction, the AC electric system, wireless-free energy sourced from the surrounding space and was even commissioned during World War 2 to design and develop anti-gravity devices and a cosmic ray engine. He said he received strange signals that he believed came from Mars while experimenting with radio at his lab.

Tesla harnessed the conductivity of electricity and was able to direct it with lightning-bolt precision, and many people witnessed his ability to conduct high-voltage electricity through his whole body so that it glowed. In 1934 the *New York Times* reported that Tesla was working on a death beam capable of knocking 10,000 enemy airplanes out of the sky.

Tesla died a poor man, with many of hundreds of patents left unfinished. It is only today with the global manufacturing and production of the electric car that Tesla's name is being rediscovered. How did someone who lived in the 1800s come up with these incredible scientific inventions? Many inventors, artists, scientists and medical intuitives have been able to reach the timeless planes or collective conscious to access future predictions. If you are able to imagine this as a possibility then you will embrace the concept of time and dreams being part of a complex phenomenon known as the Akashic records.

THE AKASHIC RECORDS

The Akashic records are a dimension of consciousness that contain a vibrational record of everything: all the human events, thoughts, words, emotions and intent ever to have occurred in the past, present or future. This also includes a record of a soul's journeys and past lives as well as a history of the cosmos. Edgar Cayce accessed his personal Akashic records (and the Akashic records of his clients and the planet) through his dreams, from which he obtained diagnostics for healing and prophetic information. He believed the Akashic records were a vibrating energy field of information that exists everywhere.

Almost every culture has acknowledged the existence of the Akashic records including the Bible, where it is referred to as the 'book of life'. They are described as a library in a non-physical plane. The Akashic records therefore exist in time, space, consciousness and energy. Our universal consciousness or higher self evolves as it experiences different situations. In time, it encodes information and emotions from past lives and present experiences that all get recorded in the Akashic field. Modern science confirms there is logic behind the theory of an all-encompassing information field. This information field is everything that has ever been and will be.

Scientist and author Ervin László gives the following scientific explanation of the Akasha:

> The paradigm emerging in science is a revolutionary innovation
> in regard to the mainstream concept of a universe where

material entities occupy separate and unique points in space and time . . . The world we observe is not the ultimate reality. It is the manifestation of a reality that lies beyond the plane of our observation . . . The Akasha is not in space and time; it is prior to the entities, laws, and constants that appear in space time . . . Contemporary physics . . . affirms the presence of a fundamental yet intrinsically unobservable plane in the world.

The Akashic records are described as being a virtual library on an etheric plane with endless books on every subject imaginable and where the unique record of every soul and its journey is kept. On those shelves is a book with your personal Akashic records, with everything you have ever been in the past, are in the present and will be in the future. They will have a chronicle your past lives and life lessons, relationship patterns, love, heartbreak, courage, anger: every word, thought, action and emotion felt as well as future possibilities that have not been manifested or may exist in parallel universes.

Accepting the concept may be difficult as science is yet to catch up with theories that are accepted by the wider community as being probable if not exact. In your dreaming minds (the subconscious and the super conscious) you experience what is not yet known to science (conscious). Astronomer and astrophysicist Carl Sagan provides this simple explanation of a non-physical plane that holds records of everything: 'The nitrogen in our DNA, the calcium in our teeth, the iron in our blood, the carbon in our apple pies were made in the interiors of collapsing stars. We are made of star stuff.' In other words, we hold the history of all life within us. Psychology counsellor Sandra Anne Taylor believes that:

The massive amounts of information in your DNA can be seen in each and every cell, but your body holds more information than that. Through the process called cellular memory, you

*hold countless records about yourself and your history – both
in this life and in long-ago existences . . . But the greatest part
of what is recorded within you is actually about you and your
eternal life – past, present, and even potential future.*

How do you access the Akashic records? Everyone has the ability
to tap into their records. When shamans journeyed through the
lower, middle and upper worlds to locate the lost soul parts and
retrieve them they passed through the Akashic field to gather
information. Cayce and other creative geniuses such as Edison, Dali
and Tesla dropped into the Akashic library through lucid dream
states, there meeting masters, teachers, guiding spirits and guidance
council who passed on information or it was shown to them in a
similar way to a hologram.

You can enter the Akashic field and read your records through
a hypnotic state using visualisation. You can replicate the lucid
dreaming state by using your active imagination. Once you are open
to discovering this form of consciousness you can explore questions
you want answers to about past lives, present situations and future
possibilities.

As our physical cells hold codes from stardust essence and
previous lifetimes (passed on from ancestral DNA), their records
form part of our energetic, etheric or astral body that re-creates itself
in each new lifetime. It is through shared human consciousness and
our emotional collective unconscious that we connect with each
other and to our environment. To begin the journey as a spiritual
navigator you will have to learn to be in an altered state, which
requires practise and knowledge. To access the Akashic records it is
recommended you work with a practitioner in this field, similar to
when you experience a past-life regression.

Here is a description of my experience in the Akashic library:

When I went to the Akashic library I was accompanied by a guide. He looked like a monk and was wearing a cassock with a hood covering his head.

I walked up a mediaeval-looking staircase to the seventh floor. That's where I intuitively felt my Akashic book was housed. When I entered the library it was like a surreal scene from a magic book or movie: it was a floating library, the books were floating in the air, and I had to jump out of my body to collect the one with my name on it.

I had asked to look at a previous life to see what I could understand about old patterns that I might repeat in the present. I saw a past life when I was a tavern owner's daughter in the Netherlands in the 1800s, married to a seaman who neglected me and when he was home treated me badly. This was an interesting insight because I have issues with relationships and trust and perhaps this was where it first began.

In this experience, although not in a sleep dream but in a hypnagogic state, the dreamer's imagery had a personal significance to her even though she may not have been aware of the connection. Sometimes in dreams figures and scenes are not simply symbolic but are part of the greater consciousness that is transcribed in the Akashic records or, perhaps more bizarrely, it is another you dreaming or living a life in a number of other universes.

As we are a total sum of past, present and future, so we all share dreams of our past lives. Dreams connected with your past lives appear to you when you are facing situations in your waking life that have a karmic link with the past. These past-life memories can help you through difficult situations and, in so doing, help you to release the karmic contracts. When you learn to identify the dream as a past-life dream and communicate with your unconscious, subconscious and super conscious minds you'll be able to use the knowledge for healing and self-awareness at a conscious level.

SIMULTANEOUS TIME

Our past, present and future exist simultaneously, but because we exist within the illusion of time the past appears to us to be in the past. Time is the thing we live our lives within and we perceive it as our eyes see it, but time is an illusion. To your higher self all of your lives are already there in their entirety, and your higher self is experiencing every moment of every single one of them right now.

NOSTRADAMUS

Past-life regressionist and hypnotherapist Dolores Cannon was contacted by the famous prophet Nostradamus through one of her patients under hypnosis. Michel de Nostredame (1503–66) was a French astrologer, physician and mystic who is best known for his book *Les Prophéties*, a collection of poetic quatrains that supposedly predicted future events. During a past-life hypnosis session Cannon's client went back to a time when she was a student of Nostradamus. The message came through that Nostradamus was looking for a link to the future because his prophecies had not been interpreted correctly and he had new ones to add. He chose Dolores Cannon to do this work and she subsequently wrote a three-volume set, *Conversations with Nostradamus,* about the translation of his famous quatrains, which contained almost 1,000 prophecies.

According to Cannon, Nostradamus named Pasteur by name, was able to give details about and dates of all the major wars including the Gulf War, and predicted the falling of the Berlin war, the break-up of the communist countries, 'metal fish' (submarines), air flight and the terrible weapon he called 'the stone in the tree' (the atomic bomb, which has been described as a mushroom cloud). He predicted our current communication as 'a world hooked together with wires': the world wide web or internet. A number of predictions are yet to happen as they are set further into the future.

The most amazing thing about this phenomenon is that Dolores Cannon reported Nostradamus telling her that communicating with him did not mean she was speaking to the dead or to a spirit floating in space. He said: 'You are speaking to me while I am alive. I am living in France writing the prophecies.' She believed she was experiencing simultaneous time.

THE TIME PHENOMENON

Time is flexible: it can stretch and expand. Think about when you hear bad news and time seems to stand still, then when you are having fun you feel time is accelerating. You may recall an occasion when you were about to have an accident and you could see yourself fall in slow motion, your mind registering what was going on but being unable to stop anything. I recall seeing my elderly mother lose her balance and fall on a hard concrete path. I was at arm's length away and all the action happened in slow motion: her staggering, me reaching to grab her but being unable to get there fast enough, her slowly falling through the air before hearing the dreaded thud of her skull hitting the ground hard. Time stood still and it seemed I had waited an hour for the ambulance to arrive as I held her down, pinching her bleeding, broken nose, when in fact it had been just six minutes.

Time is a metaphysical rabbit hole and even more so in the dream world, because it is a state where you can expand your consciousness and your understanding of the *multiverse*: the multiple levels and dimensions of reality in which time becomes elastic and ordinary rules are suspended. These understandings are at a very advanced level of dream analysis, and as an awakened dreamer it gives you the opportunity to become a co-creator of your present life and provides a new possibility for your future self.

ARE DREAMS FROM PARALLEL UNIVERSES?

Have you ever wondered about the possibility that your dreams are gateways for you to see in other realities? Your dreams could actually be reality that is happening in a parallel universe. Indigenous peoples believe that dreams are glimpses of a different world that nobody has ever visited.

According to Robert Lawrence Kuhn, if we define 'universe' as 'all there is' or 'all that exists', then by definition there can only be one universe. But if we define 'universe' as 'all that we can ever see', then many universes exist. So what is a multiverse?

Theoretically, a *parallel universe* or *alternate reality* is a self-contained, separate reality that co-exists with ours. A specific group of parallel universes is called a multiverse. Russian American physicist Andrei Linde describes multiverses as 'the entire ensemble of innumerable regions of disconnected space-time . . . a chaotic inflation which generates ever-increasing numbers of universes without end . . . the multiverse is incomprehensibly vast – and growing ever more so.'

> The universe can be divided into large regions that may have different laws of physics; not all may be suitable for life. Therefore, your life and entity are not only limited on a single earth of a single universe but on all earths of all universes.

Scientists agree that a multiverse may well exist, that there are many more universes other than our own. In that parallel world there could be a copy of you, someone who is like you in any aspects but perhaps does things differently or experiences other realities, and since time is not linear your worlds never merge. Is it possible that quantum phenomena are happening at every level of reality? As the name suggests, parallel universes exist in parallel – that is, they never touch even though they're permanently co-existing. Do you often dream of a place you've never visited, and does that place feel familiar and real to you but at the same time foreign? Maybe you see someone who also feels or looks familiar but isn't really. It may be that such a place actually exists and you are currently being visited by someone who is identical to you but isn't.

It can be a confusing concept in an age of metaphysics and quantum physics. There are people who have had prophetic dreams that have been well recorded both in modern times and in history. The most well known is the prophecy of American president Abraham Lincoln, who days before his assassination dreamed he came across a corpse covered by a cloth. He was shocked to discover that the corpse was his own. Had he experienced his death in another reality and, with it, his identical but different self in a parallel universe? During the 2020 global pandemic it appeared as though intuition was amplified due to having to tone or shut down other experiences that heightened senses such as movement and excitement in destination travel, social gatherings and celebrations, work promotions and changes and leisure activities. It could be that tapping into a range of emotions at a collective unconscious level and in the multiverse meant that more incidental prophetic dreams were being recorded.

DÉJÀ VU

Déjà vu, a French word meaning 'already seen', is a sense of repeating something that had previously happened and recognising the moment a split second before doing the previously witnessed act or event in real life. Déjà vu is that strange, sudden feeling you get when you are struck by a sense that you have done, heard or felt something before or you may have unusual memories in dreams and nightmares. About 70 per cent of people experience this sensation at least once in their lives.

Experiencing déjà vu is another explanation of how you can exist in a parallel universe with a different version of yourself, a different history and an alternate outcome than your own. In the parallel world you may have experienced the situation at one time and you are feeling it now and thinking this has happened to you before.

Science holds that déjà vu is a neurological fault between short-term and long-term memory and the hemispherical processing differences between the left and right sides of the brain, when one part of the brain processes information before the other. Sensory information takes a fast track to the limbic system, where emotional memories are associated with the event in order to prepare you for action. The slower track goes to the cognitive centres (the left logical hemisphere), where the event plus emotional memories raise your attention level so that you become aware of it. Thus you have a feeling of experiencing an event twice. The parapsychologist view, however, is related to past-life experience. If you follow the multiverse hypothesis it would make sense that you are leading parallel lives in your dreams or through your déjà vu experiences. That could explain the random nature of dreams in the way they are so much more complex than you could possibly create in your waking life.

MISREMEMBERING: THE MANDELA EFFECT

If you have ever felt convinced that something you remember to be true but then discovered you've remembered it all wrong you've experienced the *Mandela effect*. This misremembering of events or details occurs at a collective level rather than a personal level, and it first came to light when people falsely remembered that Nelson Mandela had died in prison in the 1980s when in fact Mandela passed away in 2013.

Paranormal researcher Fiona Broome coined the term 'Mandela effect' to explain this collective mistaken memory. More examples include the wicked queen in *Snow White* saying 'Mirror, mirror on the wall' rather than the correct 'Magic mirror on the wall', the robot C-3PO in *Star Wars* being all gold although he has a silver piece on his left leg, the location of the heart being the left side of the chest in anatomy diagrams. According to Broome these differences arise from the movement between the parallel realities of the multiverse, that because within each universe alternative versions of events and objects exist. Some people believe these are false memories, that much like déjà vu, they are distortions. Is it simply a glitch in time? Are people misremembering, or are they experiencing an entirely different reality?

The theory of *quantum entanglement*, which Einstein called 'spooky action at a distance', is when two particles behave as one no matter how far apart they are. When a single object shares a single wave pattern and is divided under certain conditions the parts can still be connected despite there being long distances between them. They are simultaneously and instantaneously able to communicate faster than the speed of light.

The Mandela effect and the entanglement theory both support what indigenous societies have always known: that time is circular, is playing in all dimensions at once, is an illusion and everything is interconnected. What about dreams? Dreams may simply be another form of alternate reality. I believe it's important to consider the concept of time and multiverse theories in relation to dreams because it is when we are in our altered states of dreaming that we catch a glimpse of an alternate reality in which our possible futures may be gleaned. Would that mean that the future you perceived in a dream was your future in a parallel life?

According to this hypothesis everyone is living an infinite amount of simultaneous lives. Have you ever dreamed that you were in an old situation: living at your old home, involved with a previous partner, working at an old job but in the present time? You may be comfortably off in this life but in the dream you are a beggar. You may die many times in various dreams, which may indicate that you die in some universes but not in others. It could be that there's another you living your old life.

My own dream of living another life in another place may have been a past life or one of my many lives in one of the many universes:

I was in a Tibetan village. It was very vivid; the colours of people's clothing was especially real. I followed a Tibetan woman who was making her way through the village, swerving around carts as she walked. I was dressed in black pants and black fur, which was supposed to be what a local healer there would wear. The Tibetan woman told me to follow her to a temple where I would be blessing people. That was my role in the village. It felt so right that I was doing this, as if it was my vocation.

Shamans believe that in dreaming you not only see your future but may actively choose between possible futures that are offered to you, which suggests that you become a co-creator of your world the same way that in lucid dreams you are in control of creating events and actions.

If you are open to the notion of the dream world being an alternate version of your waking world you could become more empowered to create your own future. You do this by becoming more observant of the signs in your dreams and of the synchronicities around you in your waking world. Your acts of observation create the world around you. Synchronicities increase when you become aware of them, so when you change your future you affect the collective consciousness.

You attract what you want by magnetic resonance: your thoughts and feelings have an electromagnetic signal that is sent to the quantum field, where they have the power to magnetically attract events and situations in life. By combining what you think and feel you produce a state of being that generates an electromagnetic imprint, and this imprint influences every atom in our world. You have the power to transform your reality and choose the hopes you nurture.

NEAR-DEATH EXPERIENCES

Some people who have gone through a near-death experience (NDE) claim the profound episode changed their lives as they witnessed another worldly set of events in which they were living in other realities. In an NDE the deceased initially comes out of their body into the astral plane. NDEs are quite common and exist in all cultures worldwide and happen to people of all ages; accounts of NDEs have been given by children as young as three. Around one in 10 people who die and revive have an NDE, a finding that is supported by modern research.

NDE researcher and psychology professor Kenneth Ring found some striking parallels in the out-of-body experiences people say they experienced while near death. In a 1980 study Ring found that when asked about their sense of time during an NDE only 2 per cent of respondents experienced it as normal. Six per cent reported that time seemed extended, while an overwhelming majority, 65 per cent, said they experienced no sense of time at all. The theory around time not being a reality is also a key factor here.

With conscious psychological activity present without brain function, it shows that consciousness can exist outside brain function. Many people say that they are conscious of being outside their body and floating out of their body seeing what is happening around them; they are usually looking down on their own bodies. The NDEs were described as containing a few or all of these elements: a panoramic life review where life flashes before the eyes; a journey through a dark tunnel; vision of a bright light; pleasant landscapes; and meeting a deceased friend, pet or relative or a spirit guide greeting them and a loving presence telling the soul to return as it is not their time yet.

Does an NDE change a person's life? People who have an NDE almost totally lose their fear of death, whereas people who come close to death but don't experience an NDE don't lose the fear. After having an NDE, people generally believe in some sort of afterlife. They are grateful for being alive, have a greater sense of self-worth, care more deeply for others and are able to give love more freely.

Science is yet to find a logical explanation for an NDE, just as it cannot explain cases of people dying on the operating table and being able to recall accurate details of who was in the room, what was said and even astral travelling further out to their homes then returning into their body. Consciousness persists beyond the body. Shamans describe an NDE as 'dying and coming back', as it is common in a shaman's training to reach the edge of death and return because they have to die to their former life, journey to the world of the dead and come back to assist souls in both realms of reality.

Your astral body is your subtle energetic body, the same energetic body that makes up your chakra and meridian system while in the physical body. In an astral projection, your subtle energetic body leaves the physical body and is free to explore other dimensions. In the astral plane your physical body and your astral body are connected by a silver cord, which makes it possible to return to your physical body after you wake up or come back from an NDE. In metaphysics the cord is a life thread that has a life-giving link from the higher self to the physical body, allowing the soul an ability to access and reach out into the interconnected expanses of the universe.

The most important point about an NDE is that it prepares you for dying, just as dreaming does. When you sleep you are in a watered-down version of when you die. You could remove your fear of death once you familiarise yourself with entering your dream spaces and with your personal dream topography. In the astral realm and other dimensions you may learn to become the observer and not be attached to fear, experiencing divine visitations, visions and premonitions of the future and receive guidance and discover what happens with death.

DEATH

From the point of view of the parallel universes hypothesis, death doesn't exist. If someone dies on one universe they're still alive in many others, so if there's an infinite number of universes then life is also infinite. This is why your soul or essence is considered to be immortal, a notion that may be both disturbing and comforting.

Death is not readily discussed in today's modern world, and therefore we are very poorly prepared when we encounter the deaths of friends and family. In the past when someone died there were rituals in place as an acknowledgement of death; death was visible. *Memento mori* is a Latin phrase meaning 'remember you must die'. It originated from an ancient Roman tradition in which a slave or servant had the task of standing behind a victorious general as he paraded through the streets basking in glory. The slave's sole job for the whole procession was to whisper in the general's ear continuously: 'Respice post te. Hominem te esse memento. Memento mori!' This roughly translates as 'Look behind you. Remember that you are a man. Remember that you will die.'

Memento mori became an artistic reminder of the inevitability of death. In the late Middle Ages the Black Death devastated Europe, killing around 25 million people. Out of this tragic historical event an art genre called *danse macabre* developed. Like the plague, the danse macabre was a series of art depicting kings with peasants, young with old and all manner of people to show that death comes for everyone.

Death depicted in artwork in later centuries was illustrated with a skull and other symbols such as clocks, extinguished candles, fruit and flowers. In the Victorian era it extended to the practice of photographing someone who'd recently died, usually in a pose and in dress that resembled someone living. Deceased children were often photographed with their parents and siblings, propped up on a chair so they looked very natural – this is known as 'post-mortem portraiture'. Rings engraved with skulls, known as mourning rings, were worn by everyone in the Victorian era, including Queen Victoria herself.

Locks of hair cut from the dead were worn in rings and lockets; death masks were also common. This philosophy of memento mori was a way of reflecting on one's own death in order to not take for granted the time spent in the living. Life was considered a gift and not to be wasted. Steve Jobs agreed with this view: 'Remembering that I'll be dead soon is the most important tool I've ever encountered to help me make the big choices in life . . . death is very likely the single best invention of life.'

Death in conventional dream interpretation is not related to actual death but often symbolises that a significant change or loss is occurring in a relationship or in the workplace that will result in an ending of the status quo. This change or loss is really about new beginnings, changes and transformation. Symbolic losses of your youth, opportunities, health, long-held identities and roles such as a mother's daughter or a son's father will also visit you in your dreams in the form of a death.

More clues in the dream about what aspect of you has died depend on who dies. If it's a child it could be the innocent part of you (an aspect of the self or a role you play), while if it's a friend you need to understand what that person represents to you in your waking life. If the dream is of a loved one who has passed the experience can help you to grieve and get the help you need to ease your suffering. Dreams of departed ones who come to visit are visitation dreams and are intended to provide messages, advice or guidance or even to give comfort. The spiritual elements in death dreams such as angels or bright lights can help you find hope in a dark time.

Mourning rites

In Celtic culture the banshee is a female spirit or fairy woman who heralds a death by wailing or shrieking. When someone died the banshee wailed – the same sound as that of a woman mourning and wailing – which alerted the priest to come and give the last rites. *Keening* is a Gaelic word that means 'crying'; keening women paid their respects to the deceased and expressed grief on behalf of the bereaved family. Usually performed at the wake or graveside, it was typically a dramatic vocal ritual of song, raw emotions and repeated chanting.

Irish folklore spoke of a headless rider, known as the *Dullahan*, who rode on a black horse and carried his own head. Once the Dullahan calls out the person's name he draws away the soul of his victim and the person drops dead. It was a reminder to everyone that once on their journey the deceased could not come back. Stories such as this one helped people acknowledge and make sense of death.

In previous centuries in Western cultures, black carriages and black horses with black ostrich plumes were used for adult funerals and white ones for children. Wearing black as part of the mourning dress, stopping clocks and covering mirrors were all rituals that made death more real and visible to the living. In a number of Asian countries, white mourning clothes are a symbol of purity and rebirth.

Unlike today, where we avoid preparing for death or thinking about grief, our language around death is filled with euphemisms such as 'passed', 'deceased', 'no longer with us', 'departed' and 'dearly departed'. This is quite different to the deeper meaning Australia's First Peoples give death when they talk about 'going home to country'.

Thanatophobia is the term for fear of death and dying. In Greek the word *thanatos* refers to death and *phobos* to fear. Although it's considered normal to be afraid of death, this term is a morbid or abnormal fear of death, especially one's own. Both in ancient China and ancient Greece the butterfly is the image of the spirit or soul freed from the body. Just as sleep is not merely the absence of waking, neither is death just the absence of life. Instead, it is a transformation into another state of being.

To ancient dreamers, the dream suggested a life beyond the limitation of the physical human body: an afterlife, another life. The death cults gave the ancients a sense of continuity and of commitment to their tribe or culture. The loss of these traditional death rites plays a significant part in the disruption of the smooth passage of the soul into the spirit world and prevents the mourners from expressing grief for the purpose of getting closure. More to the point, today's culture is devoted to perpetuating the lie that you can stay young forever and your life will simply go on. To remind us that we are dying on a daily basis means that we are able to prepare for death, and that is the key to entering the state of consciousness according to the Tibetan concept of the bardo state.

VISITATION DREAMS

What if you don't remember dreams of loved ones visiting? In a class I was giving on dream recall a woman asked me why she could no longer dream after being an avid dreamer all her life. I asked her how long it had been since she remembered her dreams and if there was a significant event that happened around the same time? As soon as she told me it had been 10 years prior when her husband died, I was intrigued to find out why she had shut down her ability to dream either consciously or subconsciously. Her response was rather unexpected: 'My departed husband would appear to me in my dreams and I was absolutely heartbroken to see him. I missed him so much. So I told myself one night before going to sleep that I never wanted to dream of my husband again. And I didn't.'

Setting a dream intention such as this works just as effectively as when you incubate a dream about what you would like to dream of. The woman wanted to see her husband again in her dreams now that she had had time to get over her grieving, but she could no longer recall her dreams. We worked on a series of dream techniques with dream re-entry, visualisations, incubation and setting strong intentions, and after six months she was once again able to recall her dreams, which was a great source of comfort and happiness to her.

We live in a death-avoidance culture in the West: if death is for old people, then we do our best to avoid getting old. We usually isolate the elderly when they are dying, either in aged care homes, hospices or hospitals.

The Seth Material recorded by Jane Roberts explains the after-death experience:

After-death experiences will not seem so alien or incomprehensible if you realize that you encounter similar situations as a normal part of your present existence. In sleep and dream states you are involved in the same dimension of existence in which you will have your after death experience . . . You simply turn the main focus of your attention in a different dimension of activity, one in which you have indeed continuously operated.

In other words, after death you enter another time, place and space where consciousness persists beyond the body. Dreaming, therefore, is the subconscious's preparation for dying.

Visitations from departed ones have been a primary source across the ages for the widespread belief that consciousness survives the death of the physical body. When you meet with the departed in your dreams or visions and travel beyond your physical reality into astral realms where they are at home you will find sometimes that they are dreaming of us and trying to reach us through dreams. They may want to say something they did not get a chance to say before dying, offer or receive forgiveness, bring information, provide healing or take the role of a counsellor. A number of times since he died my father has come into my dreams to give me a lecture about some personal investments he believed would not be in my best interests to commit to.

Sometimes those who've passed away need guides because they are stuck between worlds, clinging to old mindsets and unhealthy attachments. Spirits act as psychopomps and help souls move on in their new reality. The word is derived from the Greek word *psychopompos,* with *psyche* meaning 'breath', 'soul' or life' and *pompos* meaning 'conductor' or 'guide', thus a 'guide of souls'. They escort newly departed souls to the afterlife, which is represented differently in many cultures and religions.

Spirit guides and other entities show up to help if the deceased is confused and needs extra assistance. This immediate afterlife is the bardo state, or purgatory in Judeo-Christianity tradition. If we believe in existence – that you exist now and you'll always exist – then there is no 'before' or 'after' life. It is simply 'other life' or 'another form of life' that is beyond the physical realm of existence.

One of the major roles of the dream traveller when journeying to different realms is for the purpose of healing. Grief and trauma rank high on the emotional scale. It does not necessarily mean a literal death or losing someone but a loss of parts of ourselves that occurs when we have encountered something that has created a split in our soul. This then becomes a catalyst for seeking a deeper self-awareness.

Your soul, higher self or super conscious knows even more that your ego-dominated waking mind what it is you need, who you truly are and how you can best serve in the world. By bringing your awareness to and working with your dream images you can gain insights that can help you heal, open you up to neglected parts of your creative life and even help you to mend your relationships.

We are all playing the role of the oneironaut every time we enter an altered dreaming state. Hinduism and Buddhism have adopted lucid dreaming, dream yoga and yogic sleep (yoga nidra) practices to accelerate spiritual awakening. Shamans and spiritual seekers show us that dreams can be experienced in deeper, more awakened ways that open portals to other levels of reality. These portals are also known as dimensional doorways, spirit world gateways, wormholes, time tunnels and vortex accesses.

You can program your dreams to sleep on a question and wake up with an answer. You may step into your dreams and reconnect with loved ones or heal relationships or find divine visions from spirit guides. As you become more spiritually open, during dream time you will be more able to navigate beyond your five senses to the higher realms of consciousness.

Not everyone will want to have an out-of-body experience or seek out the Akashic records in the astral planes. Simply being interested in dreams and what wisdom they bring you about yourself will open your self-awareness to a higher level of consciousness. You don't need to go to sleep in order to dream. Everyday incidents will speak to you like dream symbols if you are willing to pay attention.

What enters your field of perception during the day may well have a message for you. Strange coincidences, repetitive numbers, intuition, daydreams, patterns, signs, symbols, strangeness and apparent miracles are all opportunities to being open to synchronistic moments that in turn will have an expansive effect on your deeper awareness. Stripped of distractions, you may begin to notice the beauty of small, usually insignificant things.

❖ ACTIVITY PAGE ❖

The Seth Material states that anyone can duplicate whatever results are achieved by shamans, mystics and long-time meditators simply by learning to make use of dreams. You can learn how to access and activate the full potential of your dreams on your own and bring them back to waking life for a more fully aware existence. Visualisation and dream incubation are entry points into the conscious dream world where you are aware of a deeper awakening.

DREAM INCUBATION

This is a tried and true technique that helps you to get in touch with your larger awareness. It is all about intent: by listing your intent to recall the dream and then the questions you want answers for you will be activating the principle of 'ask and you shall receive', an example of the electromagnetic vibration frequency resonance in action. To recall your dreams is not any more complex than giving yourself a suggestion before going to sleep that you will wake up as soon as a dream is completed.

◎ Relax before going to bed. Get rid of all the day's clutter from your mind so you can prepare to sleep. Do a checklist of good sleep hygiene: quiet environment, no electronic devices and no usage at least one hour before bed, warm and clean bed, no clutter and some mindfulness exercises. Remember, you will be going on a dream journey so you need to prepare your subconscious mind for the ride.

◎ State your intent in a focused manner. Repeat in your mind something like: *'Tonight in my dreams, show me how to . . . Tonight I remember/recall my dreams.'* State in the now. Summon in your dream guides – be specific, or see who shows up – and ask them to show themselves to you in your dreams.

◎ Repeat your intent three times to yourself either aloud or in your head, then write it down and put it under your pillow. This autosuggestion gesture is good for the subconscious mind: you are going to sleep on it in the sense that overnight you will have gained information that provides answers to your problems.

◎ When you make an autosuggestion for a dream recall the word acts as a trigger to recalling exactly rather than remembering imprecisely or differently. It's fascinating that when you take time to give a response to something that is important, such as signing up for a new job offer, then by going to bed and sleeping on it you are utilising both the conscious and subconscious minds and seeking involvement of the super conscious, which normally results in a more balanced outcome. There are times when your conscious critical mind is being too logical and not giving your intuition a chance to assess the situation. Your gut reaction is normally the one you should trust in decision making.

◎ Relax as you go off to sleep. Feel confident that your intent has reached your subconscious mind.

◎ If you have trained yourself to wake up after a dream in the middle of the night, focus on the dream to recall what happened and write it down briefly in your dream journal.

◎ In the morning write out each dream you recall before getting out of bed: the sooner the better. You may have many dreams, one dream or only the fragment of a dream. Never discard fragments as being unimportant as they can be a link between dream themes that sometimes go unnoticed.

The sequence of dreams is important. You might, for example, give yourself an autosuggestion to wake after your first two or three dreams and remember them. Alternatively, waken after each of your first three dreams so you can record them individually. As you delve deeper into dream work and become more at ease with the notion of parallel universes when you enter the dream space, try to remain as awake as you can be in the dream to find the differences and discrepancies between your reality and that of your dream world(s).

Pay attention to:

◎ characters you don't know in your daily life and the roles they play

◎ settings that you know well in your dream but do not exist in your ordinary waking reality

◎ colours in the dream, especially colour schemes and accent colours

◎ comparison to physical three-dimensional reality; look at what is out of place

◎ periods in history in which the dream action takes place: it may be current, your childhood, the distant past or even the future, and if it's a mix of time warps then note down how they overlap.

LIVE
THE
DREAM!

CONCLUSION

Our physical environment has a huge effect on our consciousness. This book was written during a time in history when the world was experiencing unprecedented challenges and was filled with anxiety from social changes and unrest. Old structures are being dissolved and broken up and a new energy is rising to help us reconnect with each other, with Mother Earth and with spiritual and etheric realms. When the ancients talked about being in places where the veil was thin between the worlds of the seen and unseen they were referring to both the physical and ethereal, including the borderlands of sleep where we dream.

We look to our ancestors, native wisdom traditions, the mystics and quantum physics for the reasons behind why we dream and the point of dreaming. We often forget dreams and we mostly can't make sense of them, but we all dream and we can all teach ourselves to remember them. Dreams do make sense if you learn to understand their symbols.

There are three things I feel strongly about on the topic of dreams that I hope you will heed:

◎ A dream is not 'just a dream'; we diminish the value and function of our dreams if they are reduced to this dismissive line. Never tell someone, especially a child, 'Don't worry; it's just a dream.' Allow the person to share their dream with you and, together, wonder at its mysterious structure and use the knowledge from this book to work out the message.

◎ Action is required if you want to improve anything in your existing waking life: you take lessons if you want to learn a skill, you eat well if you want to keep healthy, you exercise if you wish to be fit. You need to work to see your actions rewarded by setting the intention to dream, remembering them and writing them down on waking. If you wish to accelerate the action with techniques that take you in the astral realms of lucid dreams, out-of-body experiences and soul retrieval you need to follow set practices. Tend to your dreaming life as you would a garden. How can you expect results if it is not watered, pruned and weeded regularly?

◎ It is your response to the world around you that matters, not just at the level of the collective fear of survival as a species but from a deep knowing that comes from connection to your inner life through dreaming. Meeting your other selves in parallel universes in many disguises will provide you with the conviction and resilience to understand your waking world. And by better understanding the world you tap into humanity's indigenous knowledge systems, which are returning to the mainstream so you can better cope and thrive with the demands of a non-dreaming world.

When you are in a dream field you are connected to the energy of consciousness. In this altered state of reality you catch a glimpse of other universes, other versions of yourself including your soul or higher self. You have come to this point of understanding the value of dreams, not just for their insight but for the practice of entering other dimensions. You cannot simply be an observer of these facts and information without taking the action to bring about results: you must practise the art of dreaming. It is in practice that you will develop muscle memory with dream recall as the first principle of dream work, starting with intent.

The reward is a rich inner life filled with greater wisdom and a more awakened consciousness that is much more interconnected to the collective and to the natural world. It is in this interconnectedness you will find the resilience to create change and develop greater tolerance, and increased respect and love for the world in which you live: its inhabitants and our earth. But perhaps most of all, your journey is about knowing yourself through your dreaming life.

'We shall not cease from exploration, and the end of all our exploring will be to arrive where we started and know the place for the first time.'

— T.S. ELIOT

You are not meant to be aimlessly wandering through the astral planes of the dreamworld. Instead, you are created to be a shooting star that illuminates the firmament and all dimensions of your existence.

You are much more than you think you are.

BIBLIOGRAPHY

Although any internet references are current at the time of publication, the author and publisher cannot guaranteed that a specific location will continue to be maintained.

Academy World of Lucid Dreaming Academy, http://www.luciddreamingacademy.net/

Aspy, Denholm, National Australian Lucid Dream Induction Study 2020, http://www.adelaide.edu.au/newsroom/news/list/2020/07/20/learning-lucid-dreaming-could-help-in-isolation

awakeacademy.org

Backstrom, Kirsten, Compass Dreamwork, http://www.compassdreamwork.com

Ball, Pamela, *The Power of Creative Dreaming,* Arcturus Publishing, New York, 2006

Barrett, D., The 'committee of sleep': A study of dream incubation for problem solving, *Dreaming,* 3(2), 1993

Barrett, D., articles quoted in https://www.asdreams.org/covid-19-dreams/

Braden, Gregg, *The Divine Matrix: Bridging Time, Space, Miracles, and Belief,* Hay House, USA, 2007

Bunning, Joan, http://www.learntarot.com

Burns, Jane, Celtic Shamanism, The Shift Network, 2020, https://theshiftnetwork.com/GiftsOfCelticShamanism

Campbell, Joseph, *The Hero with a Thousand Faces,* Fontana Press, London, 1993

Cannon, Dolores, *Conversations with Nostradamus: His Prophecies Explained,* Ozark Mountain Publishing, USA, 2013

Carr, Michelle, 'How to Dream Like Salvador Dali', *Psychology Today*, 20 February 2015

cdc.gov/flu/pandemic-resources/1918-commemoration/1918-pandemic-history.htm

Clegg, Brian, *Extra Sensory: The Science and Pseudoscience of Telepathy and Other Powers of the Mind*, St Martin's Press, New York, 2013

deepluciddreaming.com

dreamstudies.org

Dumpert, Jennifer, *Liminal Dreaming: Exploring Consciousness at the Edges of Sleep*, North Atlantic Books, 2019

Elbein, Saul, 'Estonia's "holy forests" threatened by demand for biofuels', *National Geographic*, 24 August 2020

Harner, Michael, *Cave and Cosmos: Shamanic Encounters with Another Reality*, North Atlantic Books, California, 2013

Hillman, James, *The Soul's Code: In Search of Character and Calling*, Random House, New York, 1996

historytoday.com/archive/black-death-greatest-catastrophe-ever

Holecek, Andrew, *Dream Yoga: Illuminating Your Life Through Lucid Dreaming and the Tibetan Yogas of Sleep*, Sounds True, Colorado, 2016

Holecek, Andrew, Lucid Dreaming vs. Dream Yoga: What's the Difference?, http://www.andrewholecek.com/dream-yoga/

Holloway, Gillian, *The Complete Dream Book: Discover What Your Dreams Reveal About You and Your Life*, Sourcebook Inc., Illinois, 2006

Houston, Jean, *The Hero and the Goddess*, Red Wheel/Weiser,USA, 2006

Hurd, Ryan, *Lucid Immersion Guidebook: A Holistic Blueprint for Lucid Dreaming*, Dream Studies Press, 2013

Ingerman, Sandra and Wesselman, Hank, *Awakening to the Spirit World: The Shamanic Path of Direct Revelation*, Sounds True, Colorado, 2010

International Association for the Study of Dreams, http://www.asdreams.org/

Janes, Sarah, 'A Dream Cure? The Effective Healing Power of Dream Incubation in Ancient Greece', Ancient Origins, 15 December 2017

Johnson, Clare R., *The Art of Lucid Dreaming: Over 60 Powerful Practices to Help You Wake Up in Your Dreams*, Llewellyn, USA, 2020

Jung, Carl G., *The Archetypes and the Collective Unconscious*, 1955

Jung, Carl G., *Man and His Symbols*, Aldus, 1964

Kaku, Michio, *Parallel Worlds: A Journey Through Creation, Higher Dimensions, and the Future of the Cosmos*, Anchor Books, New York, 2005

Kenner, Corrine, *Tarot for Writers,* Llewellyn, USA, 2009

LaBerge, Stephen, *Lucid Dreaming: A Concise Guide to Awakening in Your Dreams and in Your Life,* Sounds True, 2009

LaMarca, Kristen, *Learn to Lucid Dream: Powerful Techniques for Awakening Creativity and Consciousness*, Rockbridge Press, California, 2019

László, Ervin and Peake, Anthony, *The Immortal Mind: Science and the Continuity of Consciousness beyond the Brain*, Inner Traditions, Vermont, 2014

Linde, Andrei, https://www.space.com/31465-is-our-universe-just-one-of-many-in-a-multiverse.html

Lipton, Bruce, *The Biology of belief: Unleashing the Power of Unconsciousness,* Matter & Miracles (10th ed.), Hay House, Australia, 2015

Lucid Dreaming Experience, http://www.LucidDreamMagazine.com

Magana, Sergio, *The Toltec Secret: Dreaming Practices of the Ancient Mexicans*, Hay House, USA, 2014

March-Smith, Rose, *Dreams: Unlock Inner Wisdom, Discover Meaning, and Refocus your Life*, DK, London, 2019

Meade, M., Holding the Thread of Life, http://www.scienceandnonduality.com

Message from White Eagle, Hopi Indigenous 16 March 2020, https://www.nativeamericanacademy.com

Modesto, Ruby and Mount, Guy, *Not for Innocent Ears: Spiritual Traditions of a Desert Cahuilla Medicine Woman*, Sweetlight Books, California, 1980

Morley, Charlie, *Lucid Dreaming Made Easy: A Beginner's Guide to Waking Up in Your Dreams*, Hay House, UK, 2018

Moss, Robert, *Conscious Dreaming: A Spiritual Path for Everyday Life*, Three Rivers Press, New York, 1996

Moss, Robert, The Power of Active Dreaming, The Shift Network, 2020, https://theshiftnetwork.com/ActiveDreamingTraining

Myss, Caroline, Breathe Together, lecture, 19 February 2020, Melbourne

Peake, Anthony, The Anthony Peake Consciousness Hour podcast, http://www.anthonypeake.com

psychologytoday.com/au/blog/dream-factory/201502/how-dream-salvador-dali

Roberts, Jane, *Seth Speaks: The Eternal Validity of the Soul*, New World Library, California, 1972

Siegel, Alan B., *Dreams That Can Change Your Life*, Berkley Publishing, New York, 1990

taileaters.com

Taylor, Sandra Anne, *The Akashic Records Made Easy: Unlock the Infinite Power, Wisdom and Energy of the Universe*, Hay House, USA, 2016

thefourwinds.com

The International Council of 13 Indigenous Grandmothers, http://www.grandmotherscouncil.org

Turner, Toko-Pa, *Belonging: Remembering Ourselves Home*, Her Own Room Press, 2017, http://www.toko-pa.com

Villoldo, Alberto, *Courageous Dreaming: How Shamans Dream the World into Being*, Hay House, USA, 2008

Waggoner, Robert, *Lucid Dreaming: Gateway to the Inner Self*, Red Wheel/Weiser, USA, 2011

Weiner, S., 'The science behind your weird corona virus dreams', *Time Magazine*, 16 April 2020

Wohlleben, Peter, *The Hidden Life of Trees: What They Feel, How They Communicate*, Black Inc, Melbourne, 2016

DREAM IT,
LIVE IT,
BE IT.

ACKNOWLEDGEMENTS

First and foremost I wish to thank my dreamers who generously gave their time in sharing their dreams with me. I am so grateful you kept a dream journal and held dreams in such high regard and importance that you recorded them for collective insights and meanings. I am sure readers will see their own dreams reflected in these insights.

I am especially grateful to industry professionals who helped me with research information and dream studies, especially author and past president of IASD, Robert Waggoner. A heartfelt thanks to my writing and research non-gender fairy godmothers who helped shaped the book and provided writing guidance, as well as kept my spirits up during prolonged periods of solitude. Helga, Angeleah, Helen, Charles, Kerrie and Linda – thanks for getting me to the finish line.

Much gratitude to the Rockpool publishers, Lisa Hanrahan and Paul Dennett, for their support and continued faith in my work.

To all my Facebook and Instagram followers and to my mind/body/spirit festival faithfuls who have attended all my talks – thank you for your encouragement.

Finally, but of greatest importance, I'd like to thank my husband Peter for his endless support and for keeping me on track during the writing of this book.

ABOUT THE AUTHOR

Rose Inserra is a successful published author and one of Australia's most popular dream researchers. Her *Dictionary of Dreams* is an international best seller and has become a trusted and practical source for those who wish to gain insight into their dreams.

Rose's love of understanding dreams as a gateway to self-awareness has led her to help many clients interpret their dreams in her capacity as a dream group facilitator. A member of the International Association for the Study of Dreams, she presents seminars, workshops and courses both in Australia and overseas and has had frequent appearances on radio and television and in magazines.

Other than her dream work, Rose is a successful children's author of over 60 books, published by leading trade and educational publishers both in Australia and internationally. She has been listed in the Notable Children's Books and short-listed for the Environment Award for Children's Literature in Australia.

Other dream-related products by Rose Inserra include *Dream Reading Cards, Dreams: What your Subconscious Wants to Tell You, Dream Journal, Sweet Dreams* mini cards and *The Gift of Dreams*.

For more information about Rose go to: www.roseinserra.com and www.rockpoolpublishing.com.au.

INDEX